100 Ideas for Teaching Communication, Language and Literacy

Continuum One Hundreds Series

100 Ideas for Teaching Communication, Language and Literacy – Susan Elkin

100 Ideas for Teaching Knowledge and Understanding of the World – Alan Thwaites

100 Ideas for Teaching Creative Development – Wendy Bowkett and Stephen Bowkett

100 Ideas for Developing Good Practice in the Early Years – Wendy Bowkett and Stephen Bowkett

100 + Ideas for Managing Behaviour – Johnnie Young

100 + Ideas for Teaching Creativity – Stephen Bowkett

100 + Ideas for Teaching Mathematics – Mike Ollerton

100 + Ideas for Teaching Thinking Skills – Stephen Bowkett

100 + Ideas for Teaching English – Angella Cooze

100 + Ideas for Teaching History – Julia Murphy

100 Ideas for Surviving Your First Year in Teaching – Laura-Jane Fisher

100 Ideas for Trainee Teachers – Angella Cooze

100 Ideas for Teaching Citizenship – Ian Davies

100 Ideas for Supply Teachers – Julia Murphy

100 Ideas for Teaching Science – Sharon Archer

100 Ideas for Teaching Geography – Andy Leeder

100 Ideas for Primary Supply Teachers – Michael Parry

100 Ideas for Essential Teaching Skills – Neal Watkin and Johannes Ahrenfelt

100 Ideas for Primary Assemblies – Fred Sedgwick

100 Ideas for Teaching Writing – Anthony Haynes

100 Ideas for Lesson Planning – Anthony Haynes

100 Ideas for Secondary School Assemblies – Susan Elkin

100 Ideas for Teaching Drama – Johnnie Young

100 Ideas for Developing Thinking in the Primary School – Fred Sedgwick

100 Ideas for Teaching

Communication, Language and Literacy

Susan Elkin

continuum

Continuum International Publishing Group

The Tower Building   80 Maiden Lane
11 York Road   Suite 704
London   New York
SE1 7NX   NY 10038

www.continuumbooks.com

British Library Cataloguing-in-Publication Data
A catalogue record for this book is available from the British Library.

ISBN: 9-780-8264-9869-8 (paperback)

Designed and typeset by Kenneth Burnley, Wirral, Cheshire
Printed and bound in Great Britain by MPG Books, Bodmin, Cornwall

Contents

Section 3: Linking Sounds and Letters

Section 4: Reading

Introduction

The Early Years Foundation Stage (EYFS) was announced by the Government in May 2007. It lays down an outline for what children under five must learn – and how they are cared for – in settings such as nurseries, nursery schools and pre-school classes.

Communication, Language and Literacy (CLL) is, of course, one of the six early learning goals. The CLL requirement of the EYFS is as follows:

> Children's learning and competence in communicating, speaking and listening, being read to and beginning to read and write must be supported. They must be provided with opportunity and encouragement to use their skills in a range of situations and for a range of purposes, and be supported in developing confidence and disposition to do so.
>
> (*The Early Years Foundation Stage, Every Child Matters: Change for Children*, DfES)

So, what does that mean for the practitioner in a setting working with babies, toddlers and young children? It means, among other things, activities and games which enhance the child's ability to use language in every way and to work towards full literacy later.

This book provides 100 ideas for such activities, organized in sections which match the six 'aspects of learning and development' for CLL laid down in EYFS:

- Language for communication
- Language for thinking
- Linking sounds and letters
- Reading
- Writing
- Handwriting.

But, of course, these sections are not watertight compartments. Young children's learning is fluid. It doesn't necessarily link to categories fixed by grown-ups. So, some of these activities would also fit – maybe with slight adaptations – into other sections too. For example, some of the activities in the 'Language for Communication' section could easily be used for 'Language for Thinking'. Some of the 'Writing' and 'Handwriting' ideas are interchangeable too. Or to put it another way, the same activity can often lead to a wide range of learning outcomes.

Value everything. Remember that gurgling and cooing are the beginning of speech. The earliest crayon marks on paper are the first steps towards writing, and hearing lots of talking voices is essential to the development of language.

Remember that at birth children are 'language neutral'. They learn to speak – and become literate in – whatever language they are exposed to. Without exposure they don't learn. So, make sure the children in your care experience as much language as possible.

I have put a suggested age range on each activity. Be aware, though, that this too is very inexact. Every child is different. A game or activity which benefits and develops one child of 18 months will also work for another who has passed his or her third birthday. Each child is unique (that's the joy of working with them) and therefore develops at his or her own rate. Many will happily embark on something at the end of the day when tiredness has set in that he or she would have rejected as babyish first thing in the morning. The given ages are intended only to be a very rough guide, and children should always be allowed to go at their own pace.

Most of the ideas need few resources; some need none. Many are, therefore, useful activities for odd moments in the day.

Ideas for things to do with children are like recipes. When an experienced, innovative cook looks at a recipe book he or she takes ideas and uses accumulated expertise to adapt them, rather than slavishly following the instructions to the letter – although many may do that too. Use this book in the same way. You may find some of these ideas work for you and your setting precisely as they are described. In other cases, you, the practitioner, will use an idea as a starting point and develop it in your own way.

The important thing is that we all work together to develop every child's CLL skills without pressure, pushing or forcing. This is why so many of the activities here are really just adult-led games which, in time, the children may quickly be able to do independently. As always, most of the learning at this stage is indistinguishable from play.

All learning – if you pitch it right – is also fun. And the more fun children (and adults!) are having the more, in general, they learn.

So experiment with the ideas and activities in this book. Personalize them and make them your own. See that the children enjoy themselves and that you all have lots of fun. Let's get our charges smiling and laughing all the way to literacy.

Section 1:
Language for Communication

Reading and Telling Stories

Age	Group size	Resources
0–5	Any, depending on age	Books at a level suitable for the child or children you are working with – picture-only books for the younger ones. You also need a fund of stories to tell (not read) in your head

Learning intentions   To make even the youngest child aware of how language is used to tell stories in readiness for reading with an instinctive understanding of how language works.

This is the most important activity of all. That is why it is first in this book. Experiencing stories is the single most important factor in eventually learning to read.

If you are reading a story from a book, sit with the child or children so that the illustrations are visible. Point to the words as you read. Don't be afraid to make up extra bits and let the children join in, although this is more difficult if you are working with more than one child.

Large format books, often known as 'Big Books' and produced by several publishers, are good for using with large groups or whole classes. The best book for a very young child is one which spreads across two laps.

If you are *telling* a story, make it as dramatic as you can with lots of gestures and eye contact. With the very young children you might base it on a toy – 'Here's Bertie the Bunny and he's going to find some carrots to eat. Look, here he goes . . .'

It is vital that children have both experiences. They must see books in use and learn that good things come out of them. They also need the communication skills which come from listening to, and watching, the face of a storyteller as opposed to a story reader.

Every child should hear several stories every day.

Taking this further

If you're reading, point to the words on the page as you read them. Get the children used to the idea that print has meaning. They will gradually start to recognize some of the word shapes. If they hear the same story often enough some will learn it by heart and then 'read' to themselves or to toys, often turning the pages at the right time. This is a good sign that he or she is on the way to literacy.

Mirroring

Age	Group size	Resources
Under 1	1:1	None

Learning intentions To make the child more aware of the sounds he or she is making and to interact conversationally with an adult. This activity will also encourage the baby to experiment with an ever-widening range of sounds.

An adult listening to, and then imitating, a baby's coos and gurgles can be the child's first conversation.

Listen to the sounds the baby makes and repeat them back to him or her. Use lots of exaggerated facial expression – smile, frown, raise your eyebrows and make eye contact.

Try to vary the sounds. If the baby makes a sound which rises, answer with one which goes down in pitch and vice versa. This is, after all, what happens in a real conversation when people ask and answer questions, or comment on what each other has said.

Obviously, mirroring can never be an exhaustive way of interacting with a baby. The child needs to hear words used conventionally too.

Taking this further

Mirroring helps to lay the foundations of real conversation. As time goes on and the child begins to make sounds like 'mum, mum, mum' you can add to this with other sounds in your answers. The more you connect with the child's face using your own expressions the more he or she will respond.

IDEA 3

Very Simple Action Rhymes

Age	Group size	Resources
0–2	Any number for most action rhymes. Some, like 'Rock a bye baby' and 'Ride a cock-horse', work best with 1:1	A book of action rhymes such as *First Picture Action Rhymes* by Felicity Brooks (Usborne Publishing Limited) or use an internet site such as Hampshire County Council www3.hants.gov.uk/action_rhymes_for_babies-2.doc/ Of course, you may have such a good bank of rhymes in your head that you don't need any reminders or resources!

Learning intentions   To make the child more aware of what words mean.

If words are linked to actions a baby is more likely to pick them up. And the actions give meaning to the words as well as being fun.

Say the rhyme as animatedly as you can with the child or children. Encourage them to join in with both words and actions.

'Pat-a-cake, pat-a-cake baker's man' is an old favourite which still works well. Or here's one you may not know:

Here is baby's face

Here is baby's chin
Here are baby's cheeks
Where smiles go out and in.
Here are baby's ears
Here is baby's nose
Here is baby's mouth
With the bubbles baby blows.
Here are baby's fingers
Here is baby's thumb
Here are baby's boots
And here is baby's bum.
Here is baby flying
High above the ground
And here is baby home again
Safe and sound.

(An original rhyme by Jack Ousbey)

Make up your own actions to this rhyme and, if you wish, substitute the child's name for 'baby.'

Taking this further

Action rhymes lend themselves to repetition. Children are often happy to say/join in the same one several times a day for weeks, which helps to reinforce the learning. If you are using a book like *First Picture Action Rhymes,* show the children the pictures and talk about them. Eventually you can lead on to more complicated action games and songs such as 'The Hokey Cokey' and 'Underneath the Spreading Chestnut Tree'.

IDEA

4

On the Phone

Age	Group size	Resources
0–2	1–3	None

Learning intentions   To get children to use talk.

Phones are part of everyday life for young children today, so phone games are a sensible way of developing language for communication in babies and toddlers.

Imitate a phone ring tone. Then say, 'There's the phone', or, 'That's my phone' and put an imaginary phone to your ear. Say, 'Hi', 'Hiya', 'Hello, or something similar and make a face as though you are listening intently. Then pretend to offer the imaginary phone to one of the children so that he or she can say hello too.

Encourage the children to take turns to make their own imaginary phone ring, answer it and then pass it to someone else for a word.

You can have great fun with different ring tones and greetings.

Taking this further

You and the children could pretend to call someone else. 'Let's phone Mrs Smith (school cook) and ask what we're having for lunch today', or, 'Shall we phone Mr Jones (headteacher) to say hello?'

Colour Game

Age	Group size	Resources
6 months –2	2–3	Coloured crayons, pieces of fabric, scraps of paper (torn from magazines perhaps) and anything else which is coloured and to hand

Learning intentions   To talk about colours to help to teach the language associated with them. It also helps to teach the colours themselves.

Children quite quickly learn to link the colours they see with the words they hear adults and other children using.

Hold up (for example) a blue crayon and say, 'This is a blue crayon.' Then show a piece of similarly coloured paper. Say, 'This paper is blue too.' Then hold up, for instance, a scrap of blue fabric or point to your shirt or something a child is wearing and say, 'And so is this.'

Encourage the children to say the colour names with you and to help you find things in the room which are the same colour as the one you are focusing on.

If the children are ready for it, get one of them to do the same thing with another colour.

Taking this further

When the children are really confident with red, blue, yellow and other basic colour words like green, brown and purple, introduce more subtle colour words such as crimson, beige, azure, amber, and so on. Bring in words such as match, dark, light, stripes, spots and pattern.

IDEA 6

Dancing with Words

Age	Group size	Resources
0–5	Whole class or any size group	A good nursery rhyme CD and a CD player

Learning intentions   To teach the shapes and sounds of words by linking them to music and rhythm.

All children have a sense of rhythm. It comes from deep inside them, even before they are born. Many experts think it relates to the pulse of the heartbeat.

Clear a big space or take the children to a hall or somewhere spacious. Play some of the tracks from the CD and get the children to move freely to the music. In the case of a baby you can dance with him or her in your arms or jiggle him on your lap. One way or another, encourage all the children to 'dance'.

Then start to say or sing the words and get the children to join in as they dance. They will probably learn very quickly the words of any rhymes they don't already know if they dance as they chant.

Taking this further

Use different and less well-known nursery rhymes. Try it with other sorts of songs too, such as numbers from musicals like Mary Poppins or Chitty Chitty Bang Bang, or folk songs.

At the Café

Age	Group size	Resources
2–3	4–5	Tables and chairs and, if available, toy plates and other crockery, dressing-up clothes and toy money. Early Vision's The Cafe Play Pack (www.earlyvison.co.uk) could provide more ideas

Learning intentions To help children to practise the sort of interactive language they hear adults using in an everyday situation.

Most children have some experience of having a drink or something to eat in a café.

Help the children to organize themselves into people using the café. Assist them to arrange the furniture as they want it. Two or three children can be customers (perhaps wearing grown-up hats or other garments); one waits at table (maybe wearing a long white shirt); another takes the money at a counter. Then they act out the situation using language such as:

- What can I get you?
- Would you like tea, coffee or orange juice?
- I'll have toast and butter and my daughter would like a currant bun.
- That'll be £2.50, please.
- Have you any egg sandwiches?
- Do you sell chapattis?
- We'll have beans on toast and pasta.
- Where are the toilets, please?
- Can I have strawberry ice cream?

❗ *Taking this further*

A simple game of 'let's pretend' can be developed into the rather more grown-up role-play. Go on building up the situation. The eaters could order and be served several courses or you could make it a self-service café so that they have to ask for what they want at a counter. Find ways to vary the situation too. It could be an Indian or Chinese restaurant or take-away, for example.

IDEA
8

I-spy with Colours

Age	Group size	Resources
1–4	4–6	None as long as you're in a fairly 'busy' room containing lots of coloured items

Learning intentions   To reinforce children's knowledge of colours and the associated words. It is also a way of getting children to interact through language.

This is fun. And it is a way in which very young children can play I-spy.

Someone – you or one of the children – says, 'I spy with my little eye something which is red (or brown or whatever).' Everyone else has to look round and make guesses. The person who guesses right gets the next turn. It may be a good idea to make the children take turns to guess so that no one gets left out. It's good training too.

Taking this further

Find items which are a mixture of colours, so you might say, 'I spy with my little eye something which is black and white (a zebra in a picture on the wall). Or, 'I spy with my little eye something which is red at the top and blue at the bottom' (a Lego model).

Phoning a Character in a Story

Age	Group size	Resources
2+	1–3	None

Learning intentions   To develop children's language by getting them to ask questions and imagine answers as they think about the stories they know.

Children who hear stories regularly become very familiar with the characters in their favourite ones.

As for Idea 3, imitate a phone ring tone. Then say, 'There's the phone' and pass the imaginary phone to a child saying something like, 'I think it's Goldilocks.' Then encourage the child to ask Goldilocks some questions such as, 'What did you have for your breakfast?' or, 'Whose bed did you go to sleep in?'

Another way of doing this is to say, 'Let's phone Cinderella and ask her what colour her party dress was/what she had for supper at the ball', or something similar. The children in the group can take it in turns to speak to the character. It's also a good way of practising sentences like, 'It's Red Riding Hood on the phone and she would like to speak to you.'

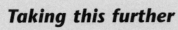

Taking this further

Get two children to pretend they are both on the phone. One is him or herself, the other is a character in a story. They make up a suitable conversation between them.

IDEA 10

Rainbows

Age	Group size	Resources
3–4	Any	Pictures of rainbows. They look really spectacular if you can project them onto an electronic whiteboard. You also need this book with the names of the colours (if you don't know them!) and the song instructions

Learning intentions   To enable children to learn the colours of the rainbow in sequence: red, orange, yellow, green, blue, indigo, violet. They also learn some new colour words (indigo) and practise fluency by singing.

Rainbows fascinate children because they are so pretty and we don't see them very often.

Talk to the children about rainbows and show them the pictures.

Sing to them – and then with them – the colours of the rainbow to the tune of 'Frère Jacques':

> Red and orange
> Red and orange
> Yellow and green
> Yellow and green
> Blue, indigo, violet
> Blue, indigo, violet
> Rainbow bright
> Rainbow bright.

(Stress the middle syllable in 'indigo'.)

Repeat this until the children have learned it, encouraging them to point to the colours in the pictures or where they can be seen in the room as they sing.

 Taking this further

The children can draw and colour their own rainbows. Any child who can manage it can label the colours or an adult could label them for him or her. Can any child think of another tune to fit the colours of the rainbow?

14

IDEA 11

Singing Everyday Language

Age	Group size	Resources
0–5	Any	None

Learning intentions To develop clear pronunciation of words, raise awareness of word sounds and rhythms and promote careful listening. The activity will also help to develop children's natural musicality.

Singing helps children to articulate words clearly and to practise the rhythm of words. It can sometimes help speech impediments such as stammering.

This is very simple provided that you, the adult, have no inhibitions about singing confidently in front of the children. Just remember that they are not music critics and will not judge you!

Instead of speaking what you want to say to the children, get into the habit sometimes of singing your words to a tune – one you know or one you've made up. Try singing things you often say such as, 'Go and wash your hands please', 'Sit down quietly', 'Who has some news to share?' Encourage the children to sing with you and/or to sing back their answers.

You can sing children's names too, especially longer ones with distinctive rhythms, such as Emily, Abdullah, Megumi or Elizabeth. You can make little tunes out of words such as elephant or crocodiles. And try singing place names such as Wellingborough, Llangollen, Inverness or whatever is relevant to your location.

Taking this further

Build up a pattern of sung questions and answers with the children. You sing a question such as, 'What would you like for pudding?' or, 'What colour are your socks?' and the child is encouraged to sing his or her answer starting on the same note that you finished on. Some older children might be able to do this in pairs too.

On the Bus

Age	Group size	Resources
2–5	At least 5	Chairs arranged to represent seats on a bus (or tram or train)

Learning intentions   To develop language, speech, confidence and imagination.

Children enjoy play based on familiar situations.

The children pretend to be passengers (families, children, elderly people) getting on the bus and sitting down. Do this with them and pretend to be one of the passengers. Initiate conversation about what you can all 'see' outside the bus. Say things like, 'Oh look, there's a man on a bicycle. What do you think he's doing?' or, 'What's that building we're passing?' As they get used to doing this, encourage the children to start the conversation themselves. It is quite fun to round off the activity by singing 'The Wheels on the Bus' together.

Taking this further

If the group is large enough, two children could be the driver and the conductor. All the passengers could address them appropriately ('Is this bus going to Norwich?', 'Two to the Market Square, please'). You can also vary the vehicle. If the children have enough experience it could be a boat on a river or an aircraft, for example.

Puppet Talk

Age	Group size	Resources
1–5	1:1	A hand puppet, doll or toy animal which can be made to move as if it is talking

Learning intentions   To develop oral confidence.

Sometimes a shy or withdrawn child will talk as, or to, a puppet when he or she finds it difficult to communicate with adults or other children.

Coax the child to talk by asking questions through the puppet. Give the puppet a put-on voice if you like. Ask anything you can think of to get a response from the child. Hold the puppet away from you and towards the child so that you are distanced from the conversation – but be aware that a shy child may not be comfortable with having anything thrust at him or her too closely. Encourage the child to operate the puppet too. The puppet can then either talk to the child or the child might talk to you through the puppet. It can even do the child's asking, 'Percy the puppet says Ellie would like a drink', for example.

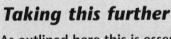

Taking this further

As outlined here this is essentially a 'special needs' activity for a child with communication problems, but nearly all children enjoy puppets and can be encouraged to use them for language work singly, in pairs or as a group, with or without adult participation.

Shopping List

Age	Group size	Resources
3–5	2 or 3. The larger the group, the harder this activity becomes	None

Learning intentions   To develop concentration and listening skills as well as practising speech.

Almost all children are taken shopping, so they will identify with, and enjoy, this memory/language development game.

Sit the children in a circle. One starts by saying, 'I went to the shops and I bought (say) a tube of toothpaste.' The next says, 'I went to the shops and I bought a tube of toothpaste – and a pair of wellies.' The third says, 'I went to the shops and I bought a tube of toothpaste, a pair of wellies – and a melon. The fourth (and you may be back to the first again by now) says, 'I went to the shops and I bought a tube of toothpaste, a pair of wellies, a melon – and a vest.'

Continue in this way until it falls apart because the children can neither add nor remember any more – by which time there will probably have been a lot of laughter. It may surprise you how long quite young children can keep this up. When it dies, simply start again. Be more specific about the shop if you like, 'I went to Sainsbury's/Morrisons/named local shop and bought . . .'

Taking this further

Use the same game but vary the situation. For example, you could play 'I went to the kitchen and I made . . .' or 'I went for a walk and I saw . . .'

Group Stories

Age	Group size	Resources
4–5	3 or 4	None

Learning intentions   To develop language use, oral skills and imagination. The activity also encourages listening.

Children who are used to hearing stories can have fun making them up in a group.

Sit the children in a circle with you. Start to tell a very simple story. For example, 'Once upon a time there was a boy named James. He lived in a house near the park with his mum, dad and dog called Bill. One day . . .' Stop and ask the child next to you to go on. When he or she has added a bit more, move on to the next child, and so on. Continue round the circle letting the story build up. Inevitably in the end it will get silly and you can all laugh about it, then you can start again. As soon as the children get the hang of the game you can get one of them to start rather than doing it yourself. You might like to go on taking a turn as the story comes round though, so that you can steer it or keep it going.

Taking this further

As children begin to grasp what a sentence is, limit them to one sentence each. Even more fun – and much more challenging – is one word each, so that they have to build the sentences by batting the words across the circle like a game of tennis. A handful of the most advanced/oldest early years children might be able to manage this.

Marching to Words

Age	Group size	Resources
2–5	Any	Words of marching rhymes

Learning intentions   To use marching rhymes and movements to reinforce word knowledge. You will also be teaching some traditional rhymes.

Moving to the rhythm of words helps the children to articulate them more clearly.

Get the children to march round the room, pretending to be soldiers, in time to the rhythm of traditional rhymes like the ones below which you all chant together:

> Hector Protector was dressed all in green.
> Hector Protector was sent to the Queen.
> The Queen did not like him.
> No more did the King.
> So Hector Protector was sent back again.

Or:

> The Grand Old Duke of York
> He had ten thousand men.
> He marched them up to the top of the hill
> And he marched them down again.
> And when they were up they were up
> And when they were down they were down
> And when they were only halfway up
> They were neither up nor down.

Taking this further

Make the rhymes into little drama games. One child could be Hector and others the king and the queen, while everyone else chants the rhyme. One child could be the Duke of York and the others the army.

Story Bags

Age	Group size	Resources
2–5	3 or 4	A bag containing three or four unexpected things such as a seashell, an orange, a knitted hat and a piece of ribbon or a shoe, a pine cone, a feather and a piece of paper with writing on it. Choose objects which look and feel interesting.

Learning intentions   To help children to shape stories using words and sentences.

Using interesting objects which the children can pass round and handle is a good way of encouraging them to use words to tell stories.

Take the objects out of the bag. Ask the children what they are and pass them round. In a group, make a story or play together based on the objects. Ask lots of questions and get as many suggestions as you can from the children. 'Who shall we pretend is wearing this hat?' 'What is his or her name?' 'Where is he?' 'Do you think he finds this seashell?' 'Where?' Keep recapping as the story builds up, and get the children to help you. Say things like, 'So once upon a time there was a girl called Alice. She put on her woolly hat to go for a walk on the beach because it was very very cold . . . Tell us what happens next, Ben.'

Taking this further

Let the children make their own story bags by choosing what to put in them. If they do this in pairs the activity will encourage discussion and more word use. Many children will also want to move on to acting out the story they have made up like a little play. They could even 'perform' it to another group.

Stories from Pictures

Age	Group size	Resources
2–5	1:1	Interesting pictures. Magazine and newspaper colour supplements (often advertisements) are a useful source. Just use them once or twice and then throw them away when they get tatty. It is very easy to find more. Look for dramatic pictures such as people pulling faces or standing somewhere odd. Adverts often feature animals or cars in unlikely situations. Pictures of houses are good too.

Learning intentions   To develop creativity and to encourage storytelling using words and sentences.

Young children can learn a lot from looking at pictures and making up stories about them.

Show the child the picture. Ask him or her simple questions about it. 'What do you think this lady's doing?' 'What is she waiting for?' 'What is she going to do next?' You can move on to other things which might be happening beyond the picture ('Are her children waiting to be picked up from school in that car?' 'What are their names?' 'Where will they sit?') If someone is pulling a face, what is he or she frightened of or laughing at? Gradually draw a 'back story' from the child to go with the picture.

> ### ! Taking this further
> Get the child you have been working with to tell another child everything he/she and you have imagined about the picture – in other words, to tell the story to someone else. It will probably come out with even more embellishments, but that's all to the good!

IDEA 19

Words with Similar Meanings

Age	Group size	Resources
4–5	3–4	A thesaurus

Learning intentions   To extend vocabulary, encourage listening and develop memory and concentration.

Children love extending their vocabulary by listing synonyms – words which have similar meanings.

Use the thesaurus as your own reference book. In advance, list or memorize adjectives such as big, large, gigantic, colossal, huge, massive, mammoth, immense, so that you can prompt the children. Sit the children in a circle and say, for example, 'Henry is a huge horse.' The child next to you has to think of another word which means the same. So he or she might say, 'Henry is a huge, gigantic horse. The next child might say, 'Henry is a huge, gigantic, massive horse' . . . and so on until you run out of synonyms. Other adjectives which work well for this include: small, hungry, frightened, surprised and tired. Obviously, you can put them in any starter sentence you like such as, 'Sammy was a small snail', or, 'Felix was a frightened boy.'

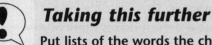

Taking this further

Put lists of the words the children think of on the classroom wall. The next time you play this you or the children can point to them. Get the children to think of other words and sentences to start the round, rather than doing it yourself.

The Doctor's Dog

Age	Group size	Resources
4–5	1–3	None

Learning intentions   To extend vocabulary and encourage concentration. The game also helps with alphabet knowledge.

Once children begin to hear the sounds which start words they can play this game.

Sitting in a circle the first person (you) says, for example, 'The doctor's dog is an active dog'. The second says, 'The doctor's dog is an awful dog', and the third says, 'The doctor's dog is an amazing dog', and so on until everyone has had a turn with adjectives beginning with 'a' to describe the dog.

Then start the next round with 'b': 'The doctor's dog is a brown dog.' 'The doctor's dog is a beautiful dog.' 'The doctor's dog is a bad dog' . . . until everyone has had a turn with every letter. Make sure everyone says the whole sentence each time, because it has a fluent rhythm (and it's quite funny).

Taking this further
The old version of this game was 'The parson's cat . . .' but few modern children know what a parson is. So, think of new variations such as, 'The postman's parrot . . .', 'The caretaker's cat . . .'

Sentence Trains

Age	Group size	Resources
4–5	Small groups or whole class	Open space, some sentences written clearly on a whiteboard or flipchart such as: Mog likes milk. Mrs Jones is our teacher. Eat more fruit.

Learning intentions   To help children learn that a sentence has a pattern and word order. It's also fun and involves moving about, discussion and cooperation.

Most children know what a train looks like; some will have ridden on one.

Show the children the board. Remind/tell them that these are called sentences. Show them the full stop at the end.

Put the children into groups of four, five or six. Each child has to 'be' one of the words in the chosen sentence. Another is the full stop. They then have to form a train by standing and holding on to each other in the right order. When they are ready the train goes round the open space with each child calling out his or her word.

Taking this further

Once they get the hang of this they can make up their own sentences and organize themselves – which provides plenty of scope for constructive talking. Make the sentences longer. Put two sentences together to make a longer train. A child will need to 'be' a conjunction such as 'and'. Try putting the train in a different order and see if it still works. For example:

Bob is our dog.

Our dog is Bob.

Is Bob our dog?

Section 2:
Language for Thinking

Jumping Beans

Age	Group size	Resources
0–3	Any	An open space for moving about and a CD player and dance CD if you like

Learning intentions   To teach or reinforce concepts of up, down, round and sideways. This is slightly abstract language, needed for thinking, which children can learn through actions.

Young children often find it difficult to take turns because they have not yet learned to wait. Here's something everyone can do together.

Go through a series of actions and get the children to follow you saying, 'We jump UP in the air', 'We jump DOWN to the ground', 'We jump ROUND' and 'We jump SIDEWAYS.' Clap your hands on the key word to emphasize it and encourage the children to do the same as they get better at the game.

You could play some cheerful dance music to jump to if you wish.

Babies and younger children can join in with a carer who either jumps with the child in his/her arms or helps the child to make the movements by supporting him/her under the armpits.

Taking this further
Add other key words (prepositions) such as out, in, along. You can also use adverbs such as quickly or slowly. It is fun to let older children take turns – if they can manage it – at leading the game rather than always doing it yourself.

Open-ended Questions

Age	Group size	Resources
2–5	1:1	None

Learning intentions To give the child the opportunity to talk at length in a guided way.

When you are trying to develop children's fluency so that they have plenty of language to think and reason with you need to think carefully about the questions you ask.

Hold a conversation with an individual child. Think of it as a very simple interview. The aim is to get the child to talk. So, do not ask 'closed' questions such as, 'What colour is your rabbit?' or, 'Is your rabbit black?' The answer to these questions is a brief 'Brown' or 'Yes'.

Get into the habit of making 'open' statements or asking open questions to invite talk. For example, try, 'Tell me about your rabbit', or, 'I'd really like to hear about your rabbit.'

Other useful questions/statements, depending on age and ability, include:

* What do think about . . . ?
* What do you like about . . . ?
* How can we . . . ?
* Why does . . . ?

The more he or she talks and the less you say, the better.

Taking this further

Make the questions more searching. Try asking things like, 'What did you notice on the journey to school today?' or, 'What do you think is the best way of doing this?'

The House that Jack Built

Age	Group size	Resources
2–5	Any	Words of the rhyme

Learning intentions   To teach language where one thing depends on another, with plenty of enjoyable rhyme and rhythm. The children will also learn new words like 'malt' and 'forlorn' and how to build long sentences.

A centuries-old rhyme is still good fun for learning the language of how one thing leads to another.

Say the rhyme with the children. Because it is very repetitive they will pick it up very quickly and chant it with you. They may like to clap their hands in rhythm too. And you can easily build in gestures (such as a square shape with hands for the house and paws up for the cat). This is how it goes:

> This is the house that Jack built.
> This is the malt that lay in the house that Jack built.
> This is the rat that ate the malt that lay in the house that Jack built.
> This is the cat that killed the rat that ate the malt that lay in the house that Jack built.
> This is the dog that worried the cat that killed the rat that ate the malt that lay in the house that Jack built.
> This is the cow with the crumpled horn that tossed the dog that worried the cat that killed the rat that ate the malt that lay in the house that Jack built.
> This is the maiden all forlorn that milked the cow with the crumpled horn that tossed the dog that worried the cat that killed the rat that ate the malt that lay in the house that Jack built.
> This is the man all tattered and torn that kissed the maiden all forlorn that milked the cow with the crumpled horn that tossed the dog that worried the cat that killed the rat that ate the malt that lay in the house that Jack built.
> This is the priest all shaven and shorn that married the man all tattered and torn that kissed the maiden all forlorn that milked the cow with the

crumpled horn that tossed the dog that worried the cat that killed the rat
that ate the malt that lay in the house that Jack built.

This is the cock that crowed in the morn that waked the priest all shaven and
shorn that married the man all tattered and torn that kissed the maiden all
forlorn that milked the cow with the crumpled horn that tossed the dog
that worried the cat that killed the rat that ate the malt that lay in the
house that Jack built.

This is the farmer sowing his corn that fed the cock that crowed in the morn
that waked the priest all shaven and shorn that married the man all tattered
and torn that kissed the maiden all forlorn that milked the cow with the
crumpled horn that tossed the dog that worried the cat that killed the rat
that ate the malt that lay in the house that Jack built.

Taking this further

Do it again – they'll love it.

Watch the Ball

Age	Group size	Resources
1–4	Any	None

Learning intentions   To teach or reinforce knowledge of words and phrases relating to place and position, such as over, under and in front of. Technically they are known as prepositions and prepositional phrases.

This is an action game you can do standing or seated in a circle.

Gather the children in a circle. Hold one flat hand up parallel to your body to make a gate. Make the other hand into a fist to represent a ball. Move the ball and say, 'My ball is under/over/beneath/on top of/in front of/beside/near/far away from (and so on) the gate.'

Say the sentence firmly each time and encourage the children to join in with both actions and words. As you change the ball's position the children will watch where it's going and try to work out which sentence goes with it.

Taking this further

Make the place words and phrases more complex and varied and don't worry if some mean the same as ones you've already had – that's the joy of English. You could use underneath, alongside, resting on, wedged under, bouncing over and many more.

If there's a child able and willing to lead sometimes instead of you, then let him or her do so.

Why?

Age	Group size	Resources
2–5	Any	A mental bank of prepared questions to adapt because, until you get really practised at this, it isn't always easy to think of suitable ones on the spot

Learning intentions   To build up language using 'Why' and 'Because' and to help children to think and talk about cause and effect.

Almost as soon as children can express themselves in words they begin to ask 'Why' questions. This is an activity to build into other work rather than to do as a specific game.

While you are working and communicating with children – say, during water play, having refreshments or making models – ask them why they are doing certain things or why something is as it is. Ask, for example:

* 'Why have you coloured this pink?'
* 'Why did you choose that chair?'
* 'Why did you want an apple today?'

Such questions invite the children to think of an answer and to start it with the word 'Because'. If you answer the 'Why' questions children ask you as carefully as you can you will have shown the children how to do it.

Be careful with your tone of voice when you ask 'Why' questions. You are asking neutrally and gently because you want to know, not because you are critical of anything the child has done. Use a pleasant voice and don't make your questions sound demanding or aggressive.

Taking this further

Start your questions with different words or phrases such as, 'What is the reason for . . . ? or, 'How do you explain . . . ?' Drop in questions beginning with other 'query' words such as 'Where' or 'Who'.

Now, Then or Later?

Age	Group size	Resources
3–5	Any	None

Learning intentions   To help children learn and use some of the everyday expressions relating to the past, present and future.

Time is a difficult concept for young children to grasp. The knowledge builds up only gradually.

Sit with children in a circle. Sing or say – and get the children to join in as a chorus – 'Today we are sitting in a group with . . .' (put in your name). Then make/sing a statement about something you did yesterday and another about something you are planning to do tomorrow.

Get the children to make their own statements beginning with 'today', 'yesterday' or 'tomorrow'. Everyone then sings or says whatever it is in chorus. Singing (see Idea 11) may be better for this than speaking because it makes each statement more of a performance and it usually means the words are more clearly enunciated.

Taking this further

Gradually introduce other time-related words and phrases such as:

- the other day
- earlier
- recently
- soon
- in a little while
- presently (which does not, of course mean 'in the present' although it did once!)
- now
- later
- in a bit
- just now.

Comparative Mouse

Age	Group size	Resources
1–5	Any	None

Learning intentions   To teach and reinforce comparative adjectives and get the children used to using them to work things out.

Movement and imagination can help to develop language for comparing.

Get the children to stand up in a loose group in an open space. Pretend there is a mouse in the class. Talk about it – what it looks like, how small it is, and so on. Give it a name if you like. Then with big gestures say, and get the children to act and chorus it with you, 'We're bigger than the mouse' (stretching up). Then repeat with, 'We're smaller than the mouse' (crouching right down on the floor). Continue with, 'We're wider/narrower/tinier/larger', and so on.

Taking this further

Introduce other comparative adjectives and invent suitable gestures and actions. Try, for instance, sillier, cleverer, tidier, hungrier and thirstier. You could also move on to superlatives – We are/ I am the biggest, smallest, widest – or play the game with a much larger imaginary animal such as a horse or an elephant.

IDEA

29

I Wonder

Age	Group size	Resources
2–5	1:1	None

Learning intentions   To encourage asking and answering thoughtful questions.

Learning phrases which encourage speculation helps with thinking.

Say to the child, 'I wonder why the sky is blue.' Or use a question of your own starting, 'I wonder if/I wonder whether/I wonder about' – or something similar. Encourage the child to give some sort of answer, and talk about it together. This sort of conversation could easily be triggered by something in a book you are looking at together ('I wonder why that rabbit is peeping of the burrow', or, 'I wonder if the washing on that line is drying'). Encourage the child to ask 'wonder' questions too. Coax him or her with prompts such as 'Do you wonder . . . ?', 'Have you ever wondered . . . ?', 'What do you wonder?' Then answer him or her as fully as you can.

Taking this further

Develop the conversation by introducing phrases such as, 'Do you think . . . ?', 'What do you think about . . . ?', 'Tell me what you think . . .', 'I'd like to know what you think about . . .'

IDEA
30

Counting

Age	Group size	Resources
0–5	Any	Words of number rhymes

Learning intentions To learn number words up to twenty through playing with rhyme.

You cannot start using counting rhymes too early. Number words are essential for thinking.

Say the number rhyme with the children using lots of eye contact and appropriate actions so that they soon begin to chant with you. Here are two traditional favourites:

> One, two, buckle my shoe.
> Three, four, knock at the door.
> Five, six, pick up sticks.
> Seven, eight, lay them straight.
> Nine, ten, a big fat hen.
> Eleven, twelve, dig and delve.
> Thirteen, fourteen, maids a-courting.
> Fifteen, sixteen, maids in the kitchen.
> Seventeen, eighteen, maids a-waiting.
> Nineteen, twenty, my plate's empty.

And,

> One, two, three, four, five,
> Once I caught a fish alive.
> Six, seven, eight, nine, ten,
> Then I let him go again.
> Why did you let him go?
> Because he bit my finger so.
> Which finger did he bite?
> This little finger on the right.

Taking this further

Try a rhyme which counts backwards and so teaches taking away or 'subtraction'. *Number Rhymes to Say and Play* by Opal Dunn (Frances Lincoln) is a good resource for this.

Cock Robin

Age	Group size	Resources
4–5	Any, but it's good to have several children to join in	The words of 'Cock Robin'

Learning intentions   To show that the language, often rhyming, makes this traditional song/poem flow along. Good 'thinking' language like 'death' is learned in a context which isn't serious.

This is an old favourite which teaches a lot of vocabulary.

Say or sing this with the children who will enjoy joining in the chorus even before they learn the verses.

Who killed Cock Robin?
I, said the sparrow,
With my bow and arrow,
I killed Cock Robin.

(CHORUS)
All the birds of the air
Fell a-sighing and a-sobbing
When they heard of the death of poor Cock Robin
When they heard of the death of poor Cock Robin.

Who saw him die?
I, said the fly,
With my little eye,
I saw him die.
(CHORUS)

Who'll dig his grave?
I, said the owl,
With my spade and trowel,
I'll dig his grave.
(CHORUS)

Who'll sing a psalm?
I, said the thrush,
As she sat on a bush,
I'll sing a psalm.
(CHORUS)

Who'll toll the bell?
I said the bull,
Because I can pull,
I'll toll the bell.
(CHORUS)

❗ Taking this further

There are many more traditional verses for 'Cock Robin'. See
www.famousquotes.me.uk/nursery_rhymes/who_killed_
cock_robin.htm or make up some new ones with the children.

Section 3:
Linking Sounds and Letters

IDEA 32

Name Sounds

Age	Group size	Resources
0–2	1:1	None

Learning intentions   To enable a very young child to begin to hear the opening of his or her name in other words.

A child's name is often the first word he or she recognizes.

Put the child's own name into sentences with other words beginning with the same sound. Make a game of it with gestures, actions, lifting, and so on, along with plenty of eye contact. Emphasize the repeated sound. For example:

*   Jamila jumps for joy.
*   Clever Chloe climbs up.
*   Liam's leaping.
*   Thomas tiptoes on his tiny toes.

Think of one or more of these for every child you work with.

Taking this further

Change the words, think of other sentences, and make them longer. Do it with other names – perhaps the name of the child's brother or sister. Or use your name: Susan sings songs.

Knee-jogging Rhymes

Age	Group size	Resources
0–2	1:1	Words of some movement rhymes

Learning intentions   To link movement and rhythm with the sounds of words.

Body movement helps babies and very young children to recognize and distinguish sounds.

Say some horseback rhymes with the baby or toddler. Here are some traditional ones you may not know:

(Hold the child on your lap facing you supported under the armpits. Jog him or her up and down as if on horseback.)

> To market, to market to buy a plum bun
> Home again, home again, market is done.

> Trit trot to Boston, trit trot to Lynn
> Take care little girl/boy – you don't fall in.

(Pretend the child falls off at the appropriate moment, and use the names of people the child knows if you like.)

> Father and Mother and Uncle John
> Went to market one by one.
> Father fell off . . . !
> Mother fell off . . . !
> But Uncle John went on and on and on and on and on.

Taking this further

Use different rhymes (see www.nurseryrhymes4u.com or www.preschoolrainbow.org).

Rhymes for Sounds

Age	Group size	Resources
0–5	Any	Words of rhymes

Learning intentions   To develop awareness of rhyme, rhythm and the sounds of words.

Almost any nursery rhyme or verse helps children to hear sounds in words.

Say the most rhythmic nursery rhymes you know repeatedly with the children who will quickly start to join in. Children learn from the rhymes at the ends of lines (cold, old), from within lines (pot, hot) and from words which start with the same sound (pease, porridge, pot), or which have the same sounds within them (like, nine). Here are three traditional rhymes which include all these features and which may be new to you.

> Pease porridge hot, pease porridge cold
> Pease porridge in the pot, nine days old.
> Some like it hot, some like it cold
> Some like it in the pot, nine days old.

> Little Miss Tucket
> Sat on a bucket
> Eating some peaches and cream.
> There came a grasshopper
> Who tried hard to stop her
> But she said, 'Go away or I'll scream.'

> Donkey donkey, old and grey
> Open your mouth and gently bray.
> Lift your ears and blow your horn
> To wake the world this sleepy morn.

Taking this further

Share as many rhymes as you can. Use a good nursery rhyme book such as *The Collins Book of Nursery Rhymes* or *The Oxford Nursery Rhyme Book* or a website such as Land of Nursery Rhymes (www.landofnurseryrhymes.co.uk) to help you find them.

Alphabet Book

Age	Group size	Resources
0–4	1:1 with under 2s or a group of 3 or 4 older children	Alphabet book

Learning intentions To teach the names and letter sounds of the 26 letters of the alphabet through association with pictures.

Even the youngest children begin to link letters and sounds if adults look at good alphabet books with them.

Look at the book with the child or children. Say both the phonic sound of the letter, as well as its name, because the children have to learn both. Talk about the pictures.

These are especially good, well-illustrated, alphabet books:

* *Eating the Alphabet* by Lois Ehlert (Red Wagon Books)
* *Alphabet Ice Cream* by Sue Heap and Nick Sharratt (Puffin)
* *ABC* by Brian Wildsmith (OUP)

Taking this further

Think with the children of other things which begin with each letter – so, if the book has 'c' for cupboard you might think of 'c' for car, cat and carpet. If the book has 'l' for lion you might come up with 'l' for light, lolly and lemon.

Make an Alphabet Frieze

Age	Group size	Resources
2–5	Whole class	Painting or colouring materials

Learning intentions   To link the sounds of the alphabet with pictures.

Every child in the group can take part in the production of this frieze.

Give each child a letter and help him or her to choose something the letter stands for and then to draw or paint it. So, the child who gets 'R' might produce a rabbit; the one with 'Q' might do a queen, and so on. When the artwork is finished, write – or help the child to write – the letter (for example, 'Rr' or 'Qq') and a label for the art (rabbit or queen) on the paper. Put these on the wall in the right order with a notice beneath saying something like 'Our Alphabet'. You probably won't have 26 children in the group so faster ones can do two or three letters.

 Taking this further

Get them to illustrate cluster letter sounds such as 'ch' for church, 'sl' for slipper or 'br' for bread.

Letters and Pictures

Age	Group size	Resources
2–4	Any	Alphabet cards or bricks. Pictures on cards – you can make these yourself or use a bought set

Learning intentions   To recognize initial sounds of words and to recognize letters when written.

This is another way to build up knowledge of the links between sounds and letters.

The idea is to get the children to match the alphabet cards to the pictures and put them together. So, a picture of a horse goes with the 'Hh' brick and a picture of an egg with the 'Ee' brick. First get the children to look at the pictures. Help them to articulate or 'spit out' the word very clearly so that they learn to hear the sound. Then look for the letter card or brick. At first the youngest children won't recognize these – an early stage of reading – so just deal with one or two each time you do the activity so that letter knowledge builds up steadily.

Taking this further
Use different pictures and do more letters at a time. In the end many four year olds will be able to match the whole alphabet to pictures.

IDEA 38

Same Sounds

Age	Group size	Resources
2–5	Any	Words of the rhymes

Learning intentions   To enable children to learn to hear and enjoy matching sounds in words.

Alliterative rhymes, often called 'tongue twisters', are fun.

Say the rhyme with the child or children. They will soon learn it with repetition. Say it slowly at first, then build up speed as they (and you!) get better at it. Here are three traditional favourites:

Peter Piper picked a peck of pickled pepper. If Peter Piper picked a peck of pickled pepper, where's the peck of pickled pepper Peter Piper picked?

Careful Katie cooked a crisp and crinkly cabbage. If careful Katie cooked a crisp and crinkly cabbage, where's the crisp and crinkly cabbage careful Katie cooked?

Betty Botter bought some butter
But, she said, this butter's bitter.
If I put it in my batter
It will make my batter bitter.
But a bit of better butter
Will make my batter better.
So she bought a bit of butter
Better than her bitter butter
And she put it in her batter
And the batter was not bitter.
So 'twas better Betty Botter
Bought a bit of better butter.

Taking this further

Make up more rhymes with the children. Lazy Maisie found a daisy . . . When Freddy was ready for bed he . . . and so on.

I-spy with Phonics

Age	Group size	Resources
2–4	4 or 5 works best so that no one has to wait too long for a turn	None. You can play this anywhere, without equipment.

Learning intentions   To encourage children to listen to spoken words and think about the sounds they begin with.

I-spy is a good old spelling favourite but it can be adapted to play with children long before they can visualize how words are written.

You say, 'I spy with my little eye something beginning with (say) "c".' Use the phonetic sound rather than the alphabet letter name. Choose items in the room which begin with a pure, hard 'c' (carrot, cat, cupboard, coat). Don't use items which happen to be spelt with a 'c' (ceiling, circle) but which begin with a different sound. At this stage avoid words like Christmas tree, crayon and cloth too, as they use more than one letter sound and may confuse the children. If it's 't' stick to toy, table or timer, not tray, thorn or throat.

Let the children guess what you are thinking of. The one who gets the right answer is the next person to say 'I spy . . .'

Taking this further

Once the children are secure with single letter sounds you can move on to playing the game with sounds made by two or more letters (phonemes) such as bridge, bread and brick, or drink, drum and dragon. 'I spy with my little eye something beginning with "br".'

Other phonemes which work well for this are 'bl', 'cl', 'fl', 'fr', 'gr', 'gl', 'pl', 'pr', 'str', 'sl', 'shr'.

Name Game

Age	Group size	Resources
2–4	Any	None

Learning intentions   To associate sounds and letters with names and build up alphabet knowledge.

It's fun to play with names – the ones which belong to people the children know and the ones they've heard in stories.

Say, 'Who can think of someone whose name starts with "A"?' (Stress the sound but mention the letter name as well. The children, prompted if necessary, might come up with Andrew, Amalia, Alan, Aunty, and so on. Then move onto 'B' (Bert, Ben, Brenda, Beverley, etc.). If the game palls and concentration flags before you reach the end of the alphabet, try doing one letter each day, or one in the morning and another in the afternoon. Then you can say, for instance, 'We'll do "F" tomorrow. See if you can think of some "F" names before then.'

Taking this further

List the names, getting the children to do some of the writing if it's appropriate. Then you have a written record of the names you have thought of – the group's own dictionary of names, in effect.

IDEA 41

Foody Alphabet Game

Age	Group size	Resources
3–5	3. With more it can be difficult to think of answers.	None. This is a good activity for odd moments such as five minutes before lunch is ready. An optional resource would be 26 cards showing the letters (lower case) of the alphabet.

Learning intentions To reinforce knowledge of the alphabet and to focus attention on the opening sounds of words.

Young children know a lot about food. With children from a range of cultural backgrounds this game is a gentle way of raising awareness of the different sorts of food friends eat.

Each person in the group takes it in turns to think of a different food beginning with 'a' (apple, adzuki bean, alfalfa, anchovy). Then move on to 'b' (beef, banana, Bovril, burger) then 'c' (chapatti, curry, cherry, chip) and so on until you get to 'y' (Yorkshire pudding, yam, yolk of egg, Yule log). It's best to leave out 'x' and 'z'.

'Food' can be as wide as you like. It can include fruit, vegetables, fish, meat, prepared dishes, brand names, and so on.

Hold up the appropriate letter during each round to remind the children and to link the visual shape to the sound.

 Taking this further

If the children are able and ready, ask them to tell the others about any food they mention which may not be familiar to all. This is a useful way of encouraging constructive talk.

Once the children can manage this activity you can narrow down the range. You could do it with, say, just fruit and vegetables, or branch away from food and do it with a completely different category such as names of people or things we wear.

Learning the Alphabet

Age	Group size	Resources
2–5	3 or 4	None

Learning intentions   To learn the alphabet in sequence.

As well as learning the sound that letters make, or combine to make, in words, young children also need to know the alphabet by its letter names.

Sing the alphabet song with the children several times until they begin to pick it up. There are several versions of it. Play a game using the alphabet song as an interlude. Child 1 has to think of the name of any animal. After she or he has said it everyone sings the alphabet song to give the next child time to think of another animal. You can probably go round the circle several times, by which time everyone will probably be quite confident with the alphabet.

Taking this further

Play the game with some other 'commodity' such as fruits or flowers.

Letter Sound Rhyme

Age	Group size	Resources
4–5	Any	Words of the nursery rhyme

Learning intentions   To learn an old alliterative rhyme with lots of unfamiliar words. It is also a number rhyme.

Here's a nice one for very able children with good vocabularies who already love playing with grown-up words.

This rhyme was popular in the nineteenth century as a family fireside game. Each person had to add a line and repeat and remember what had gone before. With twenty-first century children it is fun just to say it. Children like long words and often enjoy playing with them long before they fully understand their meaning.

> One old Oxford ox opening oysters.
> Two tired toads trying to trot to Tilsbury.
> Three thick thumping tigers taking toast for tea.
> Four finicky fishermen fishing for funny fish.
> Five frippery Frenchmen foolishly fishing for frogs.
> Six sportsman shooting snipe.
> Seven Severn salmon swallowing shrimps.
> Eight eminent Englishmen eagerly examining Europe.
> Nine nimble noblemen nibbling nectarines.
> Ten tinkering tinkers tinkering ten tin tinder-boxes.
> Eleven elephants elegantly equipped.
> Twelve typographical topographers typically translating types.

Taking this further

Make up your own version of this with the children.

Magazine Pictures

Age	Group size	Resources
2–4	2 or 3	Pile of old magazines. Newspaper weekend supplements are good

Learning intentions   To connect the initial sounds of words with correct letters.

Old magazines are a cheap and easy resource and children think it's 'grown-up' to look at them.

Say, 'Who can find me a picture of something beginning with (say) "B"?' Get the children to look through their magazines searching for babies, bags, bananas, boys, birds, and so on. Stress the sound of the letter rather than its name, but mention the name as well. Each time one child finds something suitable she/he or you can show it to the others. Advertisements are a particularly rich source of items starting with all the letters of the alphabet. When you've exhausted one letter, move on to another.

Taking this further

Older children, or those with the right motor and writing skills, could cut out and label the items they find. Build this up to a 'B' collage or an 'F' collage (for instance) to put on the wall.

IDEA
45

Beginnings and Endings

Age	Group size	Resources
3–5	2 or 3	None

Learning intentions   To develop an understanding that words can begin with the same letters that others end with.

Once children can hear the beginning sounds of words, it's time to encourage them to tune into ending sounds as well.

The idea is to build chains of words in which each word starts with the sound the previous one ended with. For example: kitchen – name – mouse – song. When you come to the end of a chain, start another one. Cat, house, room, top, twin, ball, dad, cake, book, board, Jack, bag, nan, head, hand, fruit are all good start words.

Note that when you do this orally you are using the sounds that the words end with, rather than the spelling, to encourage the children to listen. Try getting the children to take turns to think of the next link in the chain or 'brainstorm' it as a group.

Taking this further

Do it visually rather than orally, writing the words on a flipchart or whiteboard as you go. The children then look at the last letter and try to think of another word beginning with that letter. This helps with both reading and spelling.

Forming Words

Age	Group size	Resources
3–5	2 or 3	Alphabet bricks or cards

Learning intentions   To increase knowledge of the correspondence between letters and sounds to create words.

An early stage of reading and writing is to create words with letter bricks or tiles.

Make simple three-letter words by moving the bricks. Say to a child, 'Can you find a "c"?' Then, 'Let's put "o" next to it and then "t".' Finally you say, 'Look, we've made cot.' Encourage the children to move the letters around and work out/sound out what new words they've made. For example, if you change the 'c' in cot to a 'd' it becomes dot. If you change the 't' at the end to a 'd' it becomes cod, if you change the 'o' in the middle to an 'a' it makes cat. Encourage the children to experiment with the combinations. Bag is another good base word, so is pip. It doesn't matter much if some of the words the children suggest are 'made up' (such as vot, yag or mip). You are still building up literacy skills.

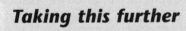

Taking this further

As the children progress, move on to making words using combined sounds such as 'br', 'cl', 'dr', 'sh', and so on. You could show children how to move letters around a screen using a computer or electronic whiteboard rather than alphabet bricks or tiles.

IDEA 47

Naming Animal Alphabet Sentences

Age	Group size	Resources
2–5	Any	None

Learning intentions To remind or teach children to hear and be aware of the sounds words start with.

Playing with words helps children to absorb the links between sounds and letters.

The idea is to find alliterative (words starting with the same sound) names for animals. So you might start with Felicity Fox. With some prompting – and probably a lot of laughter – you and the children will think of lots more such as: Henry Hare, Katie Kangaroo and Zach Zebra. The sillier the names the more fun it is (Abdullah Anteater, Yasmin Yak, Eric Elephant). You could try finding one for every letter of the alphabet.

Taking this further

Some children will be able to write the name of their animal and draw it. You can mount an animal alphabet frieze on the wall. Try building the animal name into an alliterative sentence with the children, such as Felicity Fox fought furiously or Henry Hare hurried home.

Section 4:
Reading

Books for Babies

Age	Group size	Resources
0–1	1:1	Board books, rag books or other simple books which you and the child can handle together. You don't need printed words at this stage but it doesn't matter if they are there

Learning intentions   To show that books give pleasure.

A child who is, one day, going to be a reader needs experience of books from birth.

Sit the child on your lap or next to you. Look at the book together; it is also possible to do this with the child in a baby seat. Point things out and talk about the pictures. Remember that babies absorb and understand a great deal of what is said to them long before they can speak. Let the baby hold, look at

(and probably chew!) the book. He or she is experimenting with it and finding out what a book is – and that's very healthy. Don't expect to maintain this activity for more than a minute or so, but do it several times each day.

There are many suitable books available but two particularly good ones are:

- *Faces* by John Fordham (Macmillan)
- *Mirror Me!* by Julie Aigner-Clark (Scholastic)

Taking this further

Build up the time you spend sharing the book. Try a book with more pages as concentration develops.

IDEA 49

Books Before Sleep

Age	Group size	Resources
0–1	1:1	Board book, rag book or other very simple books

Learning intentions   To show that books are gentle, pleasant things – like daytime sleeps!

Just before a nap is a good time to share a book.

Whether you are a parent, childminder or a practitioner in a nursery, if you're responsible for children under a year you will be putting them down to sleep during the day. Use a book as part of the settling down routine and then leave the book in the cot with the child. He or she then learns to associate books and bed with calm and pleasure. Ideally, put the child in the cot and sit beside him or her to look at, and talk about, the book. Otherwise, sit him or her on your lap for a minute before the nap.

Any of the books you used for Idea 48 would work well for this, but here are two more recommendations:

That's Not My Puppy by Fiona Watt and Rachel Wells (Usborne)
Baby's Day! by Beth Harwood (Templar)

Taking this further

Extend the time you spend on it. Make your comments or tiny stories slightly more elaborate.

Eyes Right

Age	Group size	Resources
0–2	1:1	Toy such as an animal or doll

Learning intentions To encourage left-to-right eye movement.

Any game which helps train a child's eye to move from left to right is useful.

Face the child. Attract the baby's or toddler's attention with the toy. Hold it where the child can see it away from you to your right (the child's left). Now shake or jiggle it across to you until it's away to your left (the child's right), making appropriate noises as you do so. Say things too like, 'Watch Billy the Goat. See he's going for a walk. There he goes!' Another way of doing this is to stand behind the child or sit him/her on your lap facing outwards and move the toy in front of the child from left to right with both of you facing in the same direction. Either way the child will watch the toy moving and his or her eyes will be led on a left-to-right journey. In English, print moves across the page from left to right. The skill to follow it does not come naturally and has to be learned. (Remember that Chinese, for example, runs from the bottom right corner of a page upwards in vertical lines and finishes in the top left corner – so Chinese children have to learn a completely different eye movement.)

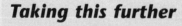

Taking this further

Put the toy in the child's hand and help him or her to move it from left to right. Of course, it isn't wrong if he or she moves a toy in any other direction, but each time you guide the child make it a left-to-right movement.

IDEA
51

Print Has Meaning

Age	Group size	Resources
0–3	1–2	Books with print

Learning intentions   To help the child to understand that print carries meaning.

Long before they can read them children need to see printed words.

Look at the book with the children. Point to the printed words as you read them aloud (but feel free to add bits of your own and to point things out in the pictures – no book is meant to be read slavishly at this level). Say things like, 'This says . . .' or, 'I'll read it to you . . .'

There are hundreds of delightful books on the market to share with under-threes. Here are four tried and tested old favourites which every generation of little ones likes:

* *Today is Monday* by Eric Carle (Puffin)
* *Each Peach Pear Plum* by Allan and Janet Ahlberg (Puffin)
* *Not Now, Bernard* by David McKee (Red Fox)
* *The Big Sneeze* by Ruth Brown (Red Fox)

Taking this further
Take the child's hand (without forcing or fussing) and help him or her to point to the words as you read them. This begins to teach him or her that, in English, print moves from left to right across the page.

Turning the Pages

Age	Group size	Resources
$1^1/_2$ upwards	1:1. With slightly older children it can work with 2	Two (or three if you have more than one child) copies of the same, very short book. Something that makes a funny noise like a bell, buzzer, hooter or whistle

Learning intentions   To teach children to turn over pages in books.

Readers learn to turn pages. So here's an idea to encourage children to do so.

Show the child that you and she/he have the same book. The game is to turn your pages together. Encourage him or her to look at the book (very grown-up!) while you read. When it's time to turn the page you make the funny noise – a signal for the child. When he or she gets it right (having listened to you reading the page and waited for the signal), give lots of praise. Most children find it fun to hear the funny noise anyway.

Try these books for this activity:

• *The Tiger Who Came to Tea* by Judith Kerr (HarperCollins)
• *Tiddler* by Julia Donaldson (Alison Green Books)

Taking this further

If you read the same book often enough the child will know exactly where the page turns come, so then he or she could control the funny noise. It's also a big step forward when you find a child 'reading' a well-known story to a toy or a younger child and turning the pages at the right moment. He or she has learned the story by heart of course, but copying adult reading behaviour is an important part of learning to read.

Picture Pairs

Age	Group size	Resources
0–3	1 or 2	Set of picture dominoes. Peter Rabbit and Friends Wooden Picture Dominoes (made by Russimco) are particularly nice, but any will do – although at this stage use a set without numbers and letters

Learning intentions   To encourage picture recognition and to develop the ability to match identical pictures.

Any game in which a child has to match pictures develops pre-reading skills.

Get the children to help you spread all the dominoes on a flat surface – perhaps the floor. You and the children make pairs or piles of matching ones. When a child picks up a domino, say something like, 'What is it? Who's that? Oh look it's Benjamin Bunny. Let's look for another domino with Benjamin Bunny.' Use a variety of words such as 'the same' and 'similar', 'match', 'another' and 'like' so that the children become familiar with the vocabulary.

Taking this further

With older children you might be able to develop this into a turn-taking game in which you see who gets the most pairs. Another variation would be to turn the dominoes face down and take turns to turn them over so that it becomes a memory game too.

IDEA
54

Picture Dominoes

Age	Group size	Resources
1–4	1 or 2	A good set of picture dominoes with initial letters – effectively alphabet dominoes

Learning intentions To develop picture and letter matching ability.

Matching pictures is a good way to build up 'looking skills'.

Get the children to help you to spread out the dominoes so that everyone can see the letters and pictures. The floor may be the best place. Each domino is, of course, double-ended and has two separate letters/pictures. So, one domino might have 'b' for banana and 'k' for kitten while another has 'q' for queen and 'w' for window. The idea is to put matching letters/pictures together. With the youngest children just use the dominoes to make linked lines – 'f'/'b' goes against 'b'/'e' which goes next to 'e'/'y', and so on. They can 'read' the pictures or the letters.

Taking this further

Older or slightly more sophisticated children may be ready to play a proper turn-taking game of dominoes in which each person has a pile of his or her own to put down and has to draw from the central pile when he or she can't 'go'. They might also be ready to move on to dominoes with whole words, using, for example, Galt's Word Dominoes.

J for Jasmine

Age	Group size	Resources
1–3	2 or 3	Sturdy cards with the initial letters of each child's name written on them boldly – one for each child in the group (if you make a stock of these you need only pull out the ones you need depending on who is in the group). Use capital (upper-case) letters for this as the letters are for the beginnings of names

Learning intentions   To help the child to learn that his or her name is connected with writing and print.

The first 'reading' most children do is focused on their own names.

The idea is for each child to find, or be helped to find, his or her 'own' letter card – so, Jack gets 'J', Ollie gets 'O 'and Maya gets 'M'. Say the sound and the letter carefully with each child, 'Yes, Jack, that's right that's "J" (alphabet name) or "J" (phonetic sound) for Jack. What is it? Say it for me . . .'

With names like Charlotte, George, Ian and Yves, which don't begin with their phonic sound, stress the letter name too. Mention the phonic sound once in passing but don't labour it.

Taking this further

Encourage the children to look for 'C' for Charlotte or 'O' for Ollie around them – on notices, in books, and so on. They could try copying the letter as part of art work too. Try the activity with any other names the child has, such as a middle name or surname.

Alphabet Brick Names

Age	Group size	Resources
1–4	2	Alphabet bricks. You will probably need two sets because many names have double or recurring letters (for example, Ella, Jonathon or Abigail). For children with the manual dexterity, and who can be trusted not to put the tiles in their mouths, an old set of Scrabble (full size version, not Travel Scrabble) is good for this because common letters are repeated within the set

Learning intentions To develop awareness that names can be written down. Letter and word recognition.

Children love creating and reading their own names.

Spread the alphabet bricks (or tiles) on a flat surface – perhaps the floor. Get the children to help you place them the right way up so that you can see the letters. Then, with the children, you look for the letters which spell their names (and perhaps yours so you are all joining in). At first they will need a lot of encouragement and help. In time they will probably be able to help each other. Draw attention to letters which are common to more than one child's name: 'Oh look here's an "s" for Sara. Let's look for another one because Lisa needs one too.' And once Connor or Allison has found one 'n' or 'l' encourage him or her to look at it carefully and then search for a second one like it.

Taking this further
Help the child to add his or her surname or, perhaps, to spell other words.

Same-letter Starts

Age	Group size	Resources
2¹/₂–4	5 or 6	A flip chart, whiteboard and markers or electronic whiteboard

Learning intentions   To build knowledge of, and confidence with, letters and how they relate to words.

This is an activity for children beginning to recognize single written letters and letter sounds.

Pick a letter such as 'h'. Articulate it very clearly and get the children to say it with you. Write it (lower case) on the chart or board. Get the children to come up and trace it with a finger or hand. Then say, 'Who can think of a word beginning with "h"?' The children begin to contribute house, hand, hello, hi, Harry in a list. When the list is as full as you can make it (and you might add a few suitable words that the children don't think of) get them to look at the words that say 'h' (for house, etc.) using the phonetic sound. You can do this with any letter. With the youngest children don't expect concentration to last for more than a minute or two, but it is an activity you can repeat quite often.

Taking this further

Gradually extend the time you spend on this. Show them that there are two ways of writing the letter – upper and lower case 'Hh' (see also Idea 58). We need the upper-case one for names like Henry or Hannah.

IDEA
58

Lower- and Upper-case Letters

Age	Group size	Resources
3–5	2 or 3	Two sets of bricks or cards, one with upper-case letters (ABCD) and the other with lower-case (abcd). Make these yourself if necessary. Use a felt-tip pen or make them in a large font on a computer, print them off and cut them up to stick on card

Learning intentions To recognize both upper- and lower-case letters and learn to pair them up.

This will help children to learn the difference between upper- and lower-case letters so that they are less likely to muddle them later.

Spread both sets of cards at random on the floor. With younger children you can use part sets such as 'A'–'F' only or 'P'–'X'. Help the children to make pairs. Say things like 'What's that you've got? Yes, it's an upper-case "D". Can you find the lower-case "d" to go with it?' Incidentally, 'upper case' and 'lower case' are the proper (printer's) terms for this difference and there's no reason why children shouldn't learn them from the beginning. Terminology like 'big' and 'small' letters is unhelpful because the difference does not depend on size. It is difference in shape that we want the child to learn to recognize.

Note: Never write words for children using upper-case letters only. ELEPHANT and CABBAGE are much harder to read than elephant and cabbage because the lower-case letters make a recognizable outline shape which the upper-case ones lack. It is worth explaining this to parents.

Taking this further

Develop this into a more formal, turn-taking game in which the children collect piles of pairs and the one with the most wins. As they begin to recognize words, draw children's attention to upper- and lower-case letters. 'Look, that's an upper-case "D" at the beginning of Durham or Darren because it's a name.'

Place Names

Age	Group size	Resources
3–5	3 or 4	Marker pens and a whiteboard. The place name cut out of newspapers and magazines or typed and printed (do it in several different sizes and fonts). Even better would be some pictures of the place name on sign posts and buildings to show on an electronic whiteboard.

Learning intentions   To encourage recognition and reading of the name of the place where the child lives.

Most children soon learn to recognize the name of their home town or area.

If you and the children live in, say, Wellingborough, Llangollen, Adelaide or Los Angeles you have a nice long name to play with and an easily recognizable word shape. But wherever you live – Ash, Ely, Ford or Deal – the children will know the word and it will often be written around them. Show them the place name. Point out its initial letter and the sound of it. Get them to trace the shape of the word with a finger – or give it to them on paper and encourage them to draw a box round the edge.

Once they're familiar with the place name show them other similar words and get them to spot the difference. For example, if you're working with Catford show them cabbage and circles occasionally. As they get better at it show them catfish and catfight.

This is reading by whole-word recognition rather than phonics. Every child needs phonics as a base, and the UK curriculum for age five and over requires that every child be taught them. However, they need some whole-word recognition skills too. Every adult reads partly by whole-word recognition. Why else is it so easy to mistake polite notice for police notice?

Taking this further

Do the activity with other local names or the county or state. So, if you're in Ludlow, look at the word Shropshire as well; if you're in Boston, look at Massachusetts. Then there's the name of your country. The children could also practise writing any of these words.

Once Upon a Time . . .

Age	Group size	Resources
4–5	3 or 4	None

Learning intentions   To build up understanding of the language used in storytelling and writing. To develop knowledge and understanding of sentence structure.

Telling stories in shared sentences makes the children more aware of how language works.

Sit in a circle. You say, 'Once upon a time there was a ——.' Let the children supply the next word, such as girl, boy, princess, man, teacher or whatever. Then say, 'She (or he) lived in a ——.' Let the children supply the word. Build up the story by inviting them to contribute one important word in each sentence. Children like doing this because it makes them feel involved, so concentration levels should be quite high. It helps with reading because they are learning the conventions of storytelling and grammar.

Taking this further

Leave more gaps for the children to fill. Let them put in more of the story, but try to make it single words that they supply, not whole sentences. That way you can keep the narrative swinging along and the children can hear and feel the rhythm of the sentences.

Room Labels

Age	Group size	Resources
0–5	Whole class	Neatly written labels and Blu-Tack to attach them. Write the labels in large letters with a felt-tip pen or use a clear, large sized computer font. Use lower-case letters

Learning intentions To get children used to associating written words with items in the room in which they spend a lot of time. To teach that print has meaning.

Getting children of all ages used to seeing print is working towards reading.

Attach labels to things in the room such as the wall, door, window and ceiling. You could also, depending on the room you're working in, label things such as the painting corner. Look around you – there should be plenty of possibilities. When you are talking to the children, point to these labels occasionally. Most children will be able to 'read' them almost as soon as they can speak. Say things like, 'What does this say?' and let them tell you. Then say, 'Yes, look, "d" for door or "w" for window' – using the phonetic sound and stressing it as you speak. This is whole-word recognition reading. If you can find anything to label which is spelled phonetically (such as desk, shelf or box), so much the better. Then you can encourage the children to sound the words out with you.

Taking this further
Label more things and get the children to make some of the labels.

Tell a Story

Age	Group size	Resources
0–5	2 or 3 with an adult if over $2^1/_2$. Otherwise 1:1	None, but you may need to think out, or look up, the story you are going to tell in advance

Learning intentions   To interest the children in stories and language and to help them to learn how stories work.

Telling a story is different from reading one and often better for the youngest children.

Tell your story to the children using as much eye contact and as many larger-than-life facial gestures as you can. You have to engage them with your eyes and your voice. If you're working with more than one child, sweep your eyes continually round the group so that no one is left out. This holds the children's attention.

Make up your story or learn and adapt one from a book. Keep it very short and simple. For example:

> 'Once upon a time there was a little brown monkey. He lived in a big tree in a forest. His name was Max. One day he jumped out of the branches and onto the ground. But there was a ravenous crocodile waiting for Max nearby, so he scampered back up his tree where it was safe. Then Max ate some bananas for his breakfast.'

Note about vocabulary: Use an occasional longish word which the children probably won't know – for example, ravenous. This is how children learn new words – by hearing them in context.

Taking this further

Build up the length of the stories you tell to extend concentration span. Get the children to make up actions to go with the story.

Read a Story

Age	Group size	Resources
$2^1/_2$–5	1–3	Story book

Learning intentions   To reinforce the concept that print has meaning and that there is pleasure to be had from words, stories and books.

Reading a story from a book you hold together helps to communicate a love of books.

Read the story to the children. Look up from the page as much as you can to make eye contact. Point things out in the pictures and encourage the children to talk about them. Point to the words as you read them too.

Try these old and new favourites:

* *10 Little Rubber Ducks* by Eric Carle (HarperCollins)
* *Rosie's Walk* by Pat Hutchins (Red Fox)
* *The Tiger Who Came to Tea* by Judith Kerr (HarperCollins)
* *Snail Trail* by Ruth Brown (Andersen Press)

> ## Taking this further
> Look for slightly longer stories with more words on a page to build up 'listening stamina' gradually. Ruth Brown's *The Old Tree* or any of Judith Kerr's Mog stories are good ones to move on to.

Serialize a Story

Age	Group size	Resources
4–5	Any, but make sure all are ready for this activity	The book or story to be serialized. Books of this sort are typically in chapters with only occasional illustrations

Learning intentions   To build vocabulary and listening ability. To experience written material slightly above the level that the child can manage independently (a child ready to enjoy being read to serially will probably already be reading words and sentences for him or herself). Serial reading is, essentially, an extension activity.

Older children are sometimes mature enough – and sufficiently sophisticated as listeners – to enjoy stories broken up into episodes read for a few minutes at a time over several days.

Read the story, looking up and making as much eye contact as possible. Dramatize it with different voices if you can and if it's appropriate to the story. Aim for 'readings' of five to ten minutes (for twenty-first century children more used to watching TV than to listening that is quite a long time to concentrate for). Try to stop at an exciting or interesting moment so that your listeners really want to hear the next 'episode'. Alternatively, use a book of short stories and use one story from the same book for each session. Try, for example:

* *Boobela and the Belching Giant* by Joe Friedman (Orion)
* *Children's Classics to Read Aloud* by Edward Blishen (Larousse Kingfisher Chambers)
* *The Puffin Book of Stories for Five-Year-Olds* by Wendy Cooling and Steve Cox (Young Puffin)

Taking this further
Look for slightly longer or more complicated books and lengthen (by a minute or two) the time you give to each episode or story.

Words with Bricks

Age	Group size	Resources
3–5	2–4	Set of lower-case alphabet bricks or tiles

Learning intentions To teach, from yet another angle, that print has meaning and that letters make words which can be read both by the person who makes the word and by others.

Using letter bricks to build words is fun and helps to develop reading skills.

Get the children to help you spread the bricks or tiles face up on the floor so that everyone can see the letters. Take three letters and form a phonetic word such as p-o-t. Say, 'Look! Who can read my word?' Help them to sound it out if necessary. Then it's a child's turn to make a word for you and the others in the group to read. You can also get extra 'mileage' out of the words by changing some of the letters. For example, once everyone has read it, change the 'p' in pot to a 'd' and say, 'Now what have I made?' Encourage the children to do this with their words too. Let them play with the bricks freely and make as many words as possible.

Taking this further

Move on from three-letter words to four- and five-letter phonetic words using consonants working together such as clap, stamp, trip, glad, thud, prod, blob, strap, fresh, or words including vowel clusters such as moon, foal, maid, meat.

Building Sentences

Age	Group size	Resources
4–5	2–4	A metal board or surface (failing all else, is there a fridge in the room? If so, use the door) and a set of magnetic words. If your setting doesn't have such a set the packets of words which come with some magnetic calendars, often given as Christmas presents, are ideal

Learning intentions   To experiment with words and find out how they can be formed into meaningful sentences which communicate something to people who read them.

Beginning to put words into a sentence for other people to read is an exciting stage in learning to read.

Spread the words on the floor or on a non-magnetic tray where the children can see and read them. Choose three or four and make a simple sentence such as, 'I like apples and oranges', by sticking the words on to the metal surface in the right order. Encourage the children to work out what you have 'written'. Then get them to make their own sentences which the rest of you have fun reading. Try changing some of the words in some of the sentences so that they say something different. For example, you could change, 'I like apples and oranges' to, 'I like swimming' or, 'Dad likes apples and oranges.'

Taking this further

Make the sentences longer and a little more complex: 'In this group we all like oranges and apples.' Point out that these are good sentences, but there is one small thing wrong with them. 'Does anyone know what? That's right. We should put an upper-case letter at the beginning.'

Reading Colour Words

Age	Group size	Resources
2–5	2–4	Items which are all one colour – for instance, a leaf, a blade of grass, green hairslide, cardigan, crayon. The word green (or whatever colour you are focusing on) written clearly in lower-case letters on a card

Learning intentions To reinforce colour knowledge and to link written colour words with their meaning.

Children love colour, and associating it with written words is another way of developing reading skills.

Talk to the children about the green (or other colour) items you have collected. Have they got any more? Can they see anything else in the room? Can they see anything green by looking out of the window? Talk about the word green. Articulate it very clearly. What does it start with? Yes, 'gr' like greedy, grape, granny and great. You might then make a green table together. Display the items with labels (can the children help with these?) and put the 'green' notice in a prominent position on the table. If you make this a weekly activity you can change the colour each week so that the children are exposed to other, different words.

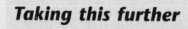

Taking this further

If some of the children are ready for it, move on to shades of colour. Introduce words such as light, pale, dark, deep and mid. Try specific words for colour shades such as azure, crimson, rosy and ochre too as a way of extending vocabulary.

IDEA
68

Mind the Gap

Age	Group size	Resources
4–5	1–2	A suitable large-print book to read aloud

Learning intentions   To use children's limited word-recognition skills in a reading activity as a way of building confidence.

Something which helps children to make sense of stories by reading words is very encouraging for learner-readers.

Read the story aloud to the children, making sure that all participants can see the printed page. As you read, point to each word as you say it (but read in a normal voice with expression and appropriate speed – don't slow up or stress every word because you're pointing at it). When you come to a word which you think the children will be able to read, stop and point so that one of them can put it in. Stop at about one word in 20. Choose short, phonetic words such as top, bat, mug, leg, Tim, or words the children have been taught to read by whole-word recognition such as the, because or though. If the child or children can't, or won't, supply the word quickly and easily, say it yourself and carry on reading – otherwise the children will lose the thread of the story and stop listening. A good book for this activity would be *Funny Stories* compiled by Michael Rosen (Kingfisher). Or try *The Kiss that Missed* by David Melling (HodderHeadline).

Taking this further
As children's reading improves you can stop slightly more often – at about one word in ten perhaps. Make this change gradually.

IDEA
69

More Work with Consonant Clusters

Age	Group size	Resources
4–5	5 or 6	Flip chart, whiteboard and markers or electronic whiteboard

Learning intentions   To build up knowledge of, and confidence with, consonant clusters.

Once children recognize most single letters and letter sounds it is time to draw attention to consonants working together to make different sounds.

Pick a consonant cluster such as 'bl'. Articulate it very clearly and get the children to say it with you. Then say 'Who can think of a word beginning with "bl"?' As the children begin to contribute blood, bleeper, blade, black, blue, blanket, blink, write the words in a list on the chart or board. When the list is as full as you can make it (and you might add a few suitable words that the children don't think of) get them to look at the words and call them out as you point to them. The children could take turns to point too. And, of course, you don't need always to read them in the order in which they are listed. You (or a child) can dot about. Other consonant clusters which work well for this include 'pr', 'str', 'fl', 'gr', 'br', 'cr', 'cl', 'dr', 'sp', 'spr'. Do one cluster a day and put the lists on display.

Taking this further

Move on to words which have the consonant cluster in the middle or at the end. For example, if you're working on 'st' include fist, last, best, tallest as well as station, stool and stop. If you are working on 'pr' include apricot and express and well as private, problem and pram.

Mini-acrostics

Age	Group size	Resources
4–5	2 or 3	Sheets of plain A4 paper and pencils or fine crayons. Colouring materials or small sticky shapes

Learning intentions   To reinforce knowledge of how names are spelled and what else you can do with the same letters – and to have fun with words.

Many adults enjoy crosswords and other word puzzles. Try getting older children interested with this simple one.

Get or help each child to write his or her name across the top of the paper ('portrait position' or narrow edge to the top). Copy the letters spaced out down the side of the paper. Then help each child to think of a word – any word – which begins with the letters of the name and write them in horizontally. For example:

L i a m	R a j	B e t h
Lion	Red	Bed
ill	alive	elephant
apple	jam	toast
mum		home

Then encourage them to colour, or otherwise decorate, their work and display it on the wall.

Taking this further

Once a child gets confident at working out acrostics based on his or her name try it with different words.

IDEA
71

Independent Reading Time

Age	Group size	Resources
4–5	Not applicable	Suitable books and quiet corners

Learning intentions   To develop reading stamina in new readers and reading behaviour in near-readers.

If they can do it, let them!

The last idea in this section is for two sorts of child. First it's for the child who cannot yet read, but understands what readers do and who likes to sit quietly looking at a book and pretending to read to him or herself or to a toy. Second, it is for the child who has actually learned to read sentences and paragraphs unaided – as a few do long before their fifth birthday. Make sure there are plenty of suitable books in the room and that there is a time and place for such children (both sorts) to do their independent reading. Don't distract them unnecessarily. You don't have to be organizing children with structured activities all the time. Just rejoice in what they are doing – it is an indication that Communication, Language and Literacy are coming on very nicely!

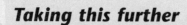

Taking this further
Supply more books. Ask the children about the books they've been reading, but don't disturb the reading to ask the question. You really learn to read by doing it (as with swimming), so the more time they spend at it the better.

Section 5:
Writing

Finger Painting

Age	Group size	Resources
0–2	1:1. This needs help and supervision	Wet, easily washable paint – powder paint mixed with water is ideal. One (bright) colour will do. Large sheets of paper – the back of old rolls of wallpaper works well. So does newspaper. Non-toxic sticky tape. Bowl of water and soap or similar

Learning intentions   To show children that you can use your fingers and paint to make marks and then look at your work and share it with others.

Making marks on paper is the very beginning of writing and it is never too soon to start.

If the child is still a baby, dip his or her hand in the paint and help him or her to make handprints on the paper.

Strap a toddler into a high or low chair with a tray or at a table. Tape the paper down so that it doesn't slip. Encourage dipping of fingers into the paint and making patterns on the paper. Most will use both hands at this stage and you will see hand prints as well as finger marks and prints. Talk about what he or she is doing and the colour of the paint.

Add the child's name to the work. Let him or her see you write it and explain what you're doing. Display it on the wall.

When the painting is finished, wash the worst of the paint off hands in the nearby bowl. Finish the job in the bathroom.

Taking this further

Children can also use feet to make prints and marks on paper, or you can let them experiment with a brush once they can hold one. Talk about the marks on the paper. Say, 'What have you painted, Jack?' It is a reminder that marks on paper can have meaning.

Fly Away Peter

Age	Group size	Resources
0–2	2–4 (or more)	A table or tray edge

Learning intentions   To help children develop finger movement and to move one finger independently of the others. It also gets them chanting in rhythm and making arm movements.

Little games like this one help to get the fingers moving ready for later writing.

You and the children put the tips of both index fingers on the edge of the table. You chant:

> Two little song birds sitting on a wall
> One named Peter, one named Paul
> Fly away Peter *(raising left finger into the air before putting it away in your lap)*
> Fly away Paul *(raising the other finger and putting it away in your lap)*
> No little song birds sitting on a wall.
> Come back Peter *(bring left finger back to the table)*
> Come back Paul *(bring the other finger back)*
> Two little song birds sitting on a wall.

You will probably want to play this several times until all the children have learned it.

Taking this further

Play the game four times using the four fingers in turn. Then get each child in the group to do it on his or her own in turns rather than doing it in a chorus.

Play a singing game with slightly more complicated actions, such as:

> Incy Wincy spider climbed up the spout *(two hands make spider climbing)*
> Down came the rain and washed the spider out *(fluttering, descending fingers become rain)*
> Out came the sun and dried up all the rain *(arms wide)*
> So Incy Wincy spider climbed up the spout again. *(as line 1)*

IDEA 74

Scribing

Age	Group size	Resources
1¹/₂–5	1:1	Large pad and a pen for you to scribe with

Learning intentions   To show that writing is useful. It also demonstrates that children's words are valuable – and it gets them talking.

When an adult records a child's ideas or words before he or she is old enough to do it this is called 'scribing'.

Encourage a very young child to tell you some news such as, 'Daddy and I went to the shop and got some milk', or, 'It's my Nan's birthday today.' A slightly older child may be able to tell you more elaborate news such as, 'We had sausages for tea. Mum got them in Sainsbury's because my Uncle Simon was coming. He likes sausages and so do I.'

Alternatively, coax out a made-up story. 'Once upon a time there was a princess. She was really scared because she heard a big noise in the night. But when her mum went to look it was just the dog knocking some plates over in the kitchen.'

Write the news or story as clearly as you can and in quite large letters on your pad.

Always add the child's name (or get him or her to do it) and make a wall display of the work.

Taking this further

Try to extend the child's work by asking questions so that he or she adds more sentences. Get two children to make up a story together. Then you could move on to a group story, where each child in a circle adds a bit to the story while you scribe it.

IDEA 75

Pretend Writing

Age	Group size	Resources
2–4	Any	Paper and pencils, felt tips or fine crayons

Learning intentions   To reinforce the concept that lines on paper have meaning, to develop motor skills needed for writing and to teach 'writing behaviour'.

Before they can write children love to pretend that lines they make on paper are writing.

Ask the child to 'write' – letters, stories, shopping lists or anything you or they can think of. Make it clear that it's a 'let's pretend' game. When they have put some marks on their paper get them to 'read' each other's writing. Start this off yourself by saying, 'What is it, Maya?' If she tells you it's a shopping list for Tesco you can then pretend to read what's on it. 'Oh yes, I see you're going to buy some oranges, a packet of biscuits and a new toothbrush, Maya.' Or if Sam tells you his is a story, you pretend to read his short story aloud. Once the other children see what you're doing they will copy by 'reading' each other's work too.

Taking this further

As the children get better at this game encourage the older or more adept ones to make their writing more like 'real' writing by making lines across the page from left to right.

IDEA 76

Writing Your Name

Age	Group size	Resources
2–4	2 or 3	Paper and pencils, felt tips or fine crayons

Learning intentions   To teach children to write their names and to give them the experience of being writers.

Most children learn to write their names before they write anything else.

Concentrate on the initial letter of each child's name to start with. Then fill in the rest of the name for him or her, using an upper-case letter to start and then lower-case letters. Gradually build up the number of letters the child can manage. Bear in mind that it can be a real effort for a young child to remember the order they come in, particularly if it's a long name. Lin will almost certainly learn to write her name more quickly and easily than Anastasia or Nicholas. So will Sam and Eva. At first make the letters very large so that they almost fill the paper. As the children become more skilled with a pencil the letters will get smaller. Big shapes are much easier for small hands to manage.

 Taking this further

Get the children to write their names on a computer (see Idea 77).

IDEA

77

First Steps on a Computer

Age	Group size	Resources
2–4	1:1	Computer (laptop or desktop) with keyboard or use an electronic whiteboard with a keyboard. A wireless keyboard is ideal because the child can easily have it at his or her own height

Learning intentions   To make the child aware of a form of writing which needs different sorts of motor and eye skills from handwriting. With older children you are also reinforcing the links between upper- and lower-case letters. Moreover, this activity is the very beginning of familiarization with the QWERTY keyboard – an essential life skill.

Using a computer is very grown-up and it makes writing very exciting.

Set the computer to a clear font and a large point size. Sit down with the child or take him or her onto your lap at the computer. Point out where the initial letter is for his or her name and let the child type it. You may need to guide his or her hand at first. A very useful piece of learning from this activity is that the letters on a QWERTY keyboard are upper case, but when you type them (unless you engage the caps lock button) they are lower case. So, the child can immediately see the connection. Try the initial letter of your name too, or that of other nearby children. Print the work to take home.

Taking this further

Work up to typing the child's whole name – and in time other things.

IDEA 78

Writing about Story Characters

Age	Group size	Resources
4–5	1 or 2	Paper, pencil, felt tips or fine crayons

Learning intentions To practise writing for a purpose and to link reading with writing.

Characters from familiar stories are good to write about.

Ask the children to think of a person or animal they know from a story such as Cinderella, Mog or anyone else you or they can think of or like. Help the children to write the name on the paper. Depending on the ability and developmental stage of each child they might:

- copy what you have written
- write the first letter and watch you write the rest
- trace the letters that you have roughed in
- write it with help with spelling
- write it unaided
- copy it from the book.

Once the name is on the paper the child can draw a picture to go with it.

Taking this further
Children who are ready to move on could write a simple sentence about the character.

Writing Emails

Age	Group size	Resources
3–5	1 or 2	A laptop or desktop computer or electronic whiteboard. A child-height wireless keyboard is ideal

Learning intentions   To make children aware of another purpose for writing and to practise forming words.

Writing and sending emails is a very grown-up activity and an important way of communicating in the twenty-first century.

If you are able to give each child a safe, controlled email address of his/her own then do so. Otherwise, use your own or one belonging to the centre or school – sending the child's message as an attachment. Get each child to think of someone to whom they would like to send a message – Mum, Dad, Nan or someone at the school or centre. You may need to organize this in advance the first time you do it so that you have the relevant email addresses to hand. Type in the recipient's address for the child and 'message from Yvie' (or Archie) in the title box. Then help the child to type his or her name with some kisses. Use a big, clear font. Then send the message.

Taking this further

Get the children to write more than their names – perhaps a sentence about what they have been doing today, or find and attach an emoticon or picture to send. You could also show them how to write very basic text messages on a mobile phone.

IDEA
80

Writing and Sending Letters

Age	Group size	Resources
2–5	2–3	A4 paper, pencils and envelopes

Learning intentions   To understand that letters contain print which has meaning and to practise writing simple ones. Letters are another 'grown-up' purpose for writing.

Sending pretend or real letters is fun and teaches children a lot.

Encourage the youngest children to make a game of 'writing' and/or drawing on the paper, putting it in an envelope and giving it to someone else saying, 'Here's a letter for you.' You could even develop this into a 'let's pretend' game in which one child takes the role of the postman and another someone at their front door. Any adult being given such a letter should, of course, make a point of opening and 'reading' it with appropriate comments. Older children can probably write at least their name on the paper and the name of the person it is for (a parent when he or she collects?) on the envelope.

Taking this further

Some older children will soon be able, with help, to set out a letter with Dear . . . first, then a sentence followed by Love from . . .

Making Notices, Labels and Signs

Age	Group size	Resources
3–5	Any	Card, pencils, marker pens and Blu-Tack, drawing pins, a staple gun or similar to mount the labels

Learning intentions   To give the children experience of writing for a real purpose and to learn that notices, labels and signs provide important information to others.

If you want notices, labels and signs in the room don't make them all yourself. Get the children to help you.

Help beginner writers to make a notice by sketching the letters very lightly on a card. Use lower-case letters except the first, which should be upper-case. Then help the child to trace over them with the marker pen. As they become more practised they may be able to do it by copying from a separate paper rather than using the guide lines. Make notices which say, for example:

- Our book corner
- Nature table
- Dressing-up box
- Sand
- Water.

You can also make labels for displays of children's work and anything else which is going on in the room.

> ## Taking this further
> Encourage the children to produce labels, notices and signs more independently as they get more practised at doing it. Some might soon even be able to make printed signs on a computer.

Writing News

Age	Group size	Resources
3–5	Any	Paper and pencils

Learning intentions   To use writing as a way of recording interesting information regularly and to understand that writing lets you do this.

Daily news writing is a classic, but enjoyable and worthwhile, early years activity.

Children share news with each other informally or they single out adults to tell things to like, 'My dad's got a new car', or, 'My hamster's had babies.' Circle time promotes news sharing too. Get them to write some of this each day. With the younger children you may have to scribe it for them (see Idea 74). Older children can be helped to write a sentence about the news themselves. Start by getting the child to work out what he or she wants to write. With less advanced children write the sentence but leave one word for the child to fill in. As they get better at this more of them will be able to write a whole sentence (or more) with help. Once the news is written you can display it on the wall, keep it in a personal folder (one for each child so that it builds up to a day-by-day diary) or send it home with the child at the end of the day.

Taking this further

Children can gradually begin to write at greater length and/or to use a computer as an alternative to handwriting.

Writing Rhymes

Age	Group size	Resources
3–5	Any	Pencils and paper, or use a computer or electronic whiteboard

Learning intentions   To increase awareness of rhyme and how words relate to each other and to practise inventing rhymes.

Most children love playing with words and it is fun to write down some of the results.

With the children, think of some boys' and girls' names to pair with rhyming adjectives. For example:

- Silly Sally
- Thirsty Kirsty
- Jolly Ollie
- Tall Paul
- Hairy Mary

Then help the children to write down the ones they've thought of. Even quite young children are often good at thinking of rhyming words, although it may be the older ones who do most of the writing. Some children may want to extend the rhyme by adding more:

- Jolly Ollie bought a lolly for his sisters, Molly and Polly.
- Tall Paul saw the ball fall.

Taking this further

Look at rhyme books with the children such as *Bobbie Shaftoe Clap your Hands* by Sue Nicholls (A&C Black) or *Chanting Rhymes* by John Foster and Carol Thompson (OUP). This will give you and them more ideas for your own rhymes.

Writing Lists

Age	Group size	Resources
$1^1/_2$–5	Any	Paper (quite small pieces are fine, even scrap paper) and pencils

Learning intentions   To practise writing for a purpose or to rehearse writing-related behaviour.

List writing is grown-up behaviour which children like to imitate.

Build making marks on a piece of paper – your shopping list – into 'let's pretend' games about shopping with the children. Say, 'Let's play shops. Now, Mrs Jones, have you got your list? What's on it today?' Or pretend to be looking at a list and collecting things from the shelf in the supermarket. For older or more advanced children help them to make a real list. Talk about what to put on it. List several items and then use it as the basis of the shopping game – ideally in several different shops.

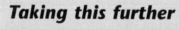

Taking this further

Most children are happy to list anything. Try activities like, 'Let's see how many animals/birds/flowers/colours we can think of and write them in a list.' Or you could ask them to list everything they have to bring to the school or centre from home each morning ('so that we don't forget anything!') or everything he or she is wearing. You could also put five or six random articles on a tray for the children to list.

Let's Make a Story

Age	Group size	Resources
4–5	Any	Pencils and paper, or use a computer or electronic whiteboard

Learning intentions To associate the words children write with stories they hear.

As children gradually master composing and/or writing skills, encourage them to try making up stories like the ones they are used to hearing.

There are three levels at which you can do this activity, depending on the developmental stage of the children. You can get children to tell stories and scribe their writing for them; get them to write single words in sentences you write; or, if they can, help them to write the sentences themselves.

The conversation might go something like this:

(You) 'What is the story about?'
(Child) 'Edward, and he's five.'
(You) 'So, shall we write, "There was once a boy called Edward who was five"?'
(Child) 'Yes, and can we say he lives in a big house near a wood?' And so on.

Once the story is finished the writer can illustrate it. You can build a story of this sort by working with a single child or make it a communal story put together by a group.

Taking this further

Each time you do this activity aim to make the story a little more complex than the time before – more sentences, more going on and more detail. Get the children to read their stories aloud to each other.

Section 6:
Handwriting

IDEA 86

Loosening Up

Age	Group size	Resources
0–3	Any	None, except music if required

Learning intentions To learn to relax and move the muscles, bones and joints in arms, wrists, hands and fingers. Eventually, freedom of movement in this part of the body will help writing.

It is fun to loosen arms, wrists, hands and fingers.

Stand or sit with the children. Say something like, 'Let's shake ourselves loose.' Hold your hands out in front of you and let them hang loosely from the wrist. Shake them from side to side. Encourage the children to join in. Then move the fingers rapidly while your hands hang. Try also shaking the lower arm from the elbow and the whole arm from the shoulder. It can help to sustain the activity for a few moments if you play some accompanying 'shaking music'. Vivaldi's 'Four Seasons' or one of Bach's 'Brandenburg concertos' work well for this – then you're raising music awareness at the same time.

Taking this further

Move on to songs and rhymes which encourage loose shaking movements such as 'The Hokey Cokey' or 'The Dingle Dangle Scarecrow':

When all the cows were sleeping
And the sun had gone to bed
Up jumped the scarecrow
And this is what he said!
 I'm a dingle, dangle scarecrow
With a flippy floppy hat
I can shake my hands like this
And shake my feet like that.
When all the hens were roosting
And the moon behind the cloud
Up jumped the scarecrow
And shouted very loud:
I'm a dingle, dangle scarecrow
With a flippy floppy hat
I can shake my hands like this
And shake my feet like that.
When the dogs were in the kennels
And the doves were in the loft
Up jumped the scarecrow
And whispered very soft:
I'm a dingle, dangle scarecrow
With a flippy floppy hat
I can shake my hands like this
And shake my feet like that. *(Repeat last four lines)*

One Finger, One Thumb

Age	Group size	Resources
0–3	Any	None, except the words of the song if needed

Learning intentions To develop free body movement – especially of the hand and arm – which eventually impacts on handwriting skill.

This is an old favourite which gets some digits moving.

Sing the song with the children, doing the appropriate actions and encouraging them to join in. The youngest children may be able to do only part of it at first or need one-to-one help from an adult.

One finger, one thumb, keep moving
One finger, one thumb, keep moving
One finger, one thumb, keep moving
We all stay merry and bright.

One finger, one thumb, one arm, keep moving
One finger, one thumb, one arm, keep moving
One finger, one thumb, one arm, keep moving
We all stay merry and bright.

One finger, one thumb, one arm, one leg, keep moving
One finger, one thumb, one arm, one leg, keep moving
One finger, one thumb, one arm, one leg, keep moving
We all stay merry and bright.

One finger, one thumb, one arm, one leg, one nod of the head, keep moving
One finger, one thumb, one arm, one leg, one nod of the head, keep moving
One finger, one thumb, one arm, one leg, one nod of the head, keep moving
We all stay merry and bright.

One finger, one thumb, one arm, one leg, stand up, sit down, keep moving
One finger, one thumb, one arm, one leg, stand up, sit down, keep moving
One finger, one thumb, one arm, one leg, stand up, sit down, keep moving
We all stay merry and bright.

Taking this further

Draw a little face on your finger and thumb tips. Use them as finger puppets. Make them speak to each other. Then let the children do the same.

IDEA

88

Let's Pretend to Write

Age	Group size	Resources
0–3	Any	Paper with crayons or felt tips

Learning intentions   To make the children aware that they can write and that writing has meaning.

Children see adults writing and imitate it long before they can form letters. Any activity – however simple – which encourages this is useful.

Let the children make marks on the paper freely. While they are doing so sit down with them and write on a piece of paper yourself – your name, perhaps or the first line of a nursery rhyme. Say something like, 'Look! I've written . . . Have you written something too? What does your writing say? Is it a letter?' Pretend to read some of each child's writing. Show the children yours and let them pretend too. Build this into make believe games about people getting and reading letters or, say, the chemist reading a prescription from the doctor. Make paper with writing 'a prop' in as many games as you can.

Taking this further

Gradually, older children can be encouraged to make marks on the paper which actually look like pretend writing – left-to-right lines across the paper, perhaps.

Dog Leads

Age	Group size	Resources
1–3	2 or 3	Crayons or felt tips. Photocopied sheets on which you have drawn or transferred a row of dogs down the left-hand side and a corresponding row of posts down the right. On a piece of A4 paper put about four of each

Learning intentions   To teach the children to draw lines from left to right and to encourage motor skills for later writing.

Left-to-right writing movement has to be learned by all children growing up in a European culture, wherever they are in the world.

Ask the children to draw the dog leads and tie each dog to its post. They should start with the dog and draw the lead from left to right across the page. Then they can colour the dogs, colour the posts and decorate the paper in other ways too.

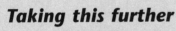

Taking this further

Design other 'worksheets' which need a left-to-right line. It could, for example, be a spider casting a thread towards a leaf to make a web, or a boy throwing a rope over a wall. If any of the children are beginning to develop higher level pencil skills, get them to draw a collar on the dog to attach the lead to and to loop the lead round the post. They could think of names for the dogs too.

'S' for Snake

Age	Group size	Resources
1–3	Any	None

Learning intentions   To teach the shape of the letter S and link it with its sound.

'S' is a lovely letter to play games with because it's so curvy.

Stand with the children. Say something like, 'Let's make an "S" for Sssssammy the Ssssssnake.' Then draw one in the air in a single line with big arm

movements from high above your head sweeping down to low on the ground. Make sure you get it the right way round for the children – if you're facing them you will need to do it backwards; if you are standing with them, do it conventionally. Get them to join in until you are all making big 'S' shapes (and incidentally doing a bit of stretchy PE). Then you can all hissssss, like Sssssammy the Sssssnake.

! Taking this further

Think of other 's' words to link the shape to, such as soap, school, slipper, sausage. Adapt the game for other letters. You can make 'X' or 'Y' with your whole body, for example, or curve round to be a 'C', or draw an 'M' in the air.

Scissors

Age	Group size	Resources
3–4	1:1	A pile of old magazines or colour supplements, scissors, glue (such as Pritstick), sheets of paper

Learning intentions To develop hand skills and coordination, partly in preparation for writing; also, incidentally, to teach scissors rules such as always pointing scissors downwards, passing them to someone else handles first and putting them away safely when finished with.

Manipulating scissors is another good way of developing finger skills which help with writing.

The child leafs through the magazines looking for a picture he or she likes. Advertisements are a particularly good source of bright and cheerful images. Then, with help if necessary, he or she cuts it out and glues it onto the paper. The child might choose to put several cut-outs on one piece of paper or just one large one. Supervise the use of the scissors carefully (that's why this is a one-to-one activity) and emphasize how scissors should be handled safely to make sure no one gets hurt.

Taking this further

Aim for smaller pictures to cut out so that it takes more dexterity. Work up to using the cut-outs to make a proper collage.

Writing One-line Letters

Age	Group size	Resources
2¹/₂–5	1 or 2	Paper and pencils, felt tips or crayons. Handwriting book if you need it

Learning intentions To teach children to form letters from lines rather than linking a circle and line to form 'b' 'd' 'p', and so on.

Learning to form letters from continuous flow lines is important.

Practise this yourself in private first if you need to. Lower-case letters 'a', 'b', 'd',' g', 'p' and 'q' do not consist of a 'ball' and a 'stick' added separately as many children were taught in the past. Work out a way of forming them without lifting the pencil from the paper or consult a good handwriting book such as *Teach Yourself Better Handwriting* by Rosemary Sassoon and Gunnlaugur S. E. Briem (Teach Yourself books). Help the children to form these letters. Use big movements and make the letters large enough to fill a sheet of A4 paper so that the children really get the feel for the shape and how to create it. And give them lots of practice. They can decorate their work afterwards, of course.

Taking this further

Move on to 'h', 'e', 'm', 'w' and 'y'. The aim, remember, is to form each letter from a continuous line. Ideally, each letter should have a hook (or serif) so that it is ready to be joined to the next letter.

Holding the Pencil

Age	Group size	Resources
3–5	1 to 2	Range of pencils, felt tips, crayons, pens and paper. Possibly specially shaped handwriting pencils (see below)

Learning intentions To teach children to hold their pencils in a relaxed way which works towards eventually forming letters easily and with control.

Use writing at all levels to help the child to develop a natural, comfortable way of holding a pencil or pen.

Provide a selection of writing implements and let each child choose what suits him or her best. Some small hands are happier with a fat barrel; others prefer something more slender. Triangular, barrelled pencils with a groove in which the index finger rests work well for some children. Encourage the children to write – a single letter, a name, a letter to grandma, or whatever. If they are very young and/or immature it will be 'pretend' writing or patterns. If they are beginning to read and form letters, then that's all to the good. Remember that pencil grip develops through three stages:

- The basic palmar grasp, where the child wraps all his or her fingers round the pencil and moves the whole arm to make marks.
- The digital finger grasp, where the hand is above the pencil and the child uses the whole arm to manipulate it.
- The tripod grasp, with fingers placed near the tip of the pencil with the thumb opposing the fingers, and movement controlled by the fingers.

The last stage is what you're aiming for. Encourage it, but don't force it.

Taking this further
Encourage the children to write several letters to form a word, or several words to form a sentence.

Choosing and Positioning Paper

Age	Group size	Resources
3–5	Any	Different sorts of paper – rough, shiny, coloured, grained. If you have a variety of colours it's even better

Learning intentions   To make children aware of the paper they are using.

Getting the right paper in the right place matters for beginner-writers.

Let each child try out each sort of paper with some 'writing' (pattern, 'pretend' letters, words, it doesn't matter). Which do they like best? Which is nicest to work on? Different children will respond in different ways, but most find they can make marks more easily on slightly textured paper rather than on a glossy surface, especially if they are using a felt tip. Talk to them too about where they put the paper. For a right-handed child it should be slightly to the right of the centre of the body and for a left-hander, to the left. Some children like it slightly angled. If the paper is on the 'wrong' side the child has to lean across his or her own body to reach it and that's awkward. Discuss all this very gently so that the child begins to think about it. Have fun and don't force it until the child is ready.

Taking this further

Encourage the children, as part of language development, to use expressions like, 'I prefer grainy paper for my writing', 'I find it hard to write/draw on shiny paper', 'I like my paper straight', 'I am right/left-handed.'

Loopy Patterns

Age	Group size	Resources
3–5	1 or 2	Writing implements and paper (see Ideas 92 and 93). Music if you like

Learning intentions   Making patterns can help to loosen a child's writing hand.

Turn pattern-making into a game. Join in with a piece of paper of your own. Show the child the patterns you want him or her to make on the paper. Make the patterns loopy, moving from left to right across the paper. Try zig-zags too. Have scribbly fun. Give them different colours to work with and encourage them to cover the paper. Play some cheerful music if it helps.

Taking this further

Develop as many loopy patterns for children to play with as you can.

Controlling the Pencil

Age	Group size	Resources
4–5	2–3	Range of pens and pencils and paper with different textures

Learning intentions   To develop the control of writing implements.

Children who are ready can practise more formal patterns.

Sit down with the children at a table. Make sure that the tables and chairs are at a suitable height for the children so that they can sit comfortably to write/draw without stretching or hunching. Let them choose a writing implement and piece of paper (see Ideas 93 and 94). Encourage them to think about how they position the paper. Now work on patterns which help to develop pencil control such as the loops and zig-zags they experimented with in Idea 95. Join in yourself and let them see that you are having fun too. Let them colour and otherwise decorate their work (perhaps with stickers or stars).

Taking this further

Invent more patterns to practise. Sustain the activity for longer as concentration span grows. Talk to the children about any letters they can see in their patterns (see Idea 97).

Forming Letters

Age	Group size	Resources
4–5	2 or 3	Writing implements in different colours. Paper in different textures and colours

Learning intentions   To help children to form and recognize letters based on their patterns.

Letters can emerge from patterns.

Encourage the children to make loopy patterns on their paper such as the ones in Idea 96.

Help the children to find letters in their work and to put rings round them. For example, a row of loops might look like the letter 'l' or zig-zags might look like an upper-case 'M'. Then talk about words which begin with those letters and get the children to draw pictures to illustrate the letter.

Taking this further

Use other patterns and other letters. As the child gets better at forming letters you can make a pattern of a row of joined-up letters, but take care with how you form them. Aim for a continuous line. Use a good handwriting manual (see Idea 92) for advice if you need help.

IDEA 98

Something for Left-handers

Age	Group size	Resources
2–5	Any	None, unless you use music

Learning intentions   To teach left and right and to make children aware of right-handedness and left-handedness. To develop finger, arm and other movements.

About ten per cent of the population is left-handed. A game which gives the left-handed child an advantage is fun and good for his/her self-esteem.

Stand in a ring with the children. Put up your left hand. Ask them all to put up theirs. Tell them to put the right hand behind their backs. Then move the fingers on the left hand one by one. Then clench and unclench it, or rotate it from the wrist. Wave. Beckon. Now do some pointing games with the left hand. Let's all point at the window. Let's all point at the door/floor/ceiling. Then try standing on the left foot. Or stand on the right and point with the left. Make the game as physical as you can, with music if you like. Use the terms 'left' and 'right' and get the children to chorus with you. You may want to stand with your back to the children so that your left and right is the same as theirs.

Taking this further

Get one of the children to lead the game and call out, or mime, instructions.

Tips for helping left-handed writers:

- Try angling the paper about 45 degrees to the right.
- Aim for a good 'three-point grip' between the thumb, index and middle fingers.
- Keep the hand and wrist under the writing/drawing line.
- Try a sloped writing surface.

Joining It Up

Age	Group size	Resources
4–5	4	Writing implements and paper in different textures and colours

Learning intentions   To practise writing cursively.

Many handwriting experts now recommend that children be encouraged to join their letters as soon as they start to write.

Show each child how to write his or her name in joined-up writing using, wherever possible, a continuous line. Some will be ready for this before they complete the Foundation Stage, especially if they have learned to form letters using continuous lines with a hook on each and they have had plenty of practice with flowing patterns. Start with an upper-case letter which probably won't join the rest. Write the rest of the word in lower-case letters.

Taking this further

Build up whole sentences in cursive writing. Make some of your classroom notices in cursive writing so that the children get used to seeing it. Use it sometimes when you write words for them to copy.

Upper-case Letters

Age	Group size	Resources
4–5	3 or 4	A laptop or desktop computer or an electronic whiteboard – ideally with a wireless keyboard so the children can use it at the right height for them

Learning intentions   To have fun using a computer and to teach or reinforce the difference between upper-case and lower-case letters. To develop motor skills needed to type a letter or two.

Children have to learn that each letter has two forms.

Set the computer to a good clear font such as Arial or Times New Roman and on a large point size such as 20pt. Type a lower-case letter such as 'm'. Get the children to identify it and link it with a word such as mummy, mouse or melon. Then get one of them to hold the shift key and type 'm' again to get an upper-case 'M' next to your lower-case one. Do this with as many letters as the children can concentrate on – perhaps two or three a day. Remember that they are improving their computer skills as well as their writing and reading. It is an activity worth doing every day with children who are ready for it.

Taking this further

Reverse the activity by starting with an upper-case letter and getting them to fill in the lower-case equivalent. Or get them to type names which need an upper-case letter to start – their own, other children's names in the group, the town or village, the name of the school or centre, and so on.